MOON SPELLS FOR BEGINNERS

YOUR COMPLETE GUIDE TO THE HIDDEN POWER OF LUNAR PHASES, WICCAN MAGIC, RITUALS, AND WITCHCRAFT

FRANK BAWDOE

© Copyright 2021 - All rights reserved.

It is not legal to reproduce, duplicate, or transmit any part of this document in either electronic means or in printed format. Recording of this publication is strictly prohibited and any storage of this document is not allowed unless with written permission from the publisher except for the use of brief quotations in a book review.

Disclaimer: Any medicinal benefits given here are a product of my own research and as such should not be taken over the advice of trained medical professionals. Always make sure that anything you consume is 100% safe. If you are pregnant, consult your doctor or midwife before consuming something you haven't tried before.

CONTENTS

Introduction	7
1. MOON MAGIC ESSENTIALS	9
Mother Moon and Her Power and Symbolism	10
Association of Deities With the Power and Energy of the Moon	16
The Moon and the Triple Goddess	20
Creative Pull and Influence of the Moon	23
The Symbolism of the Moon Phases	26
New Moon	26
New Moon: Magical Practices for a New Moon:	27
Crescent Moon	28
Waning Crescent Moon	29
Waxing Crescent Moon	31
First Quarter Moon	33
Gibbous Moon	35
Full Moon	36
Disseminating Moon	40
Last Quarter Moon	42
Balsamic Moon	44
Special Moon Phases	45
Blood Moon	45
Super Moon	46
Blue Moon	50
Dark Moon	52
Lunar Eclipse	54

2. MOON SPELLCASTING: COMMON TOOLS AND PREPARATION … 57
   Moon Altars … 58
   Moon Magic With Herbs, Flowers, and Plants … 70
   Formula for Writing Out Intention … 83
   Preparing for Moon Spells … 87
   Ritual Practices for Each Moon Phases … 89

3. NEW MOON SPELLS … 91
   New Moon Spells, Rituals, and Ceremonies … 92
   Attracting a Lover Spell … 92
   New Romance Spell … 94
   Facilitating Love Spell … 95
   Fertility Spell … 97
   Authenticity Spell … 98
   Job Hunting Spell … 99
   New Moon Divination Spell … 101
   Adventurous Spell … 102

4. WAXING CRESCENT MOON SPELLS FOR TAKING ACTION … 105
   Bathe Me in Confidence Spell … 106
   Passion Over the Moon Spell … 106
   Grant Me Patience Spell … 108
   I Made the First Move Spell … 109
   Conflict Resolution Spell … 111
   Energy Cleansing Ritual … 112
   Enemy Protection Spell … 114

5. FIRST QUARTER MOON SPELLS FOR MAKING DECISIONS … 117
   Sacred Water Ritual … 118
   Healthy Habits Spell … 119
   Mental Clarity Spell … 120
   Make the Right Decision Spell … 122
   Pivot Spell … 124
   To Tell the Truth … 125

6. WAXING GIBBOUS MOON SPELLS FOR GETTING SPECIFIC	127
Waxing Gibbous Ritual	128
Personification Spell	129
Communication Spell	130
Positivity Spell Jar	132
Inspirational Moon Spell	133
Reclaim Personal Power Spell	134
Prosperity Spell	136
Strengthen My Love Spell	137
7. FULL MOON SPELLS FOR CELEBRATION, GLOW, AND REFLECTION	141
Smoke Cleansing Ritual	142
Dream Vision Spell	142
Ritual Steps for Harvesting Full Moon Bliss	144
Lunar Rejuvenation Spell	145
Self-Love Celebration Spell	146
8. WANING GIBBOUS MOON SPELLS FOR EXPRESSING GRATITUDE	149
Embracing Obstacles Spell	150
Honor Thy Anger Spell	151
Honoring a Relationship Spell	152
Thanksgiving Ritual During Waning Gibbous Moon	153
Minimalism Moon Spell	154
Thanking Mother Earth Spell	155
9. WANING CRESCENT MOON FOR SURRENDER AND RELEASE	159
Dark Goddess Ritual	160
Banish My Alcohol Addiction Spell	161
You Need to Cut the Cord Spell	163
Final Thoughts	167
References	169

SPECIAL BONUS!

Thank you for adding this book to your Wiccan Library! To learn more, join Frank's Wiccan Community and get this additional free *Wicca Starter Kit* book 100% FREE!

Hundreds of others are already enjoying insider access to all of my current and future full-length books, 100% free! If you want insider access plus this free *Wicca Starter Kit* book, all you have to do is **click the link below** to claim your offer!

INTRODUCTION

It is no secret that witches love Mother Moon and that learning how to harness lunar powers can amplify your magic and help you manifest amazing spells. Witches and non-witches alike, most of us feel a connection to the moon. For Wiccans, the moon represents the mother or feminine energy, and the sun represents the father or masculine energy. I remember being in elementary school and feeling a great sense of comfort in the moon and being amazed that it was so present, yet so far away.

Almost every culture has deities corresponding with our Moon, which should come as no surprise since the Moon's position in the sky heralds the change in seasons. The word lunar is derived from the Latin word *Luna*, which is feminine. The Moon has influenced human behavior since the start of humankind. Unlike the Sun, the Moon has a differential pull, meaning that its gravitational pull on the Earth is strongest on the side facing the moon. This is what causes the tides. Two-thirds of the human body is water, so if the moon can shift the waters in the oceans, it can

INTRODUCTION

certainly influence the fluids and chemicals in our body, affecting behavior. Moon magic is undoubtedly one of Nature's greatest forces and assists Wiccans and non-witches in using lunar energy to practice magic. For Wiccans, the magic of the Moon provides a more powerful connection with the Goddess and all that she has in store for you. The moon not only charges your crystals, candles, oils, and herbs, it charges you!

I am looking forward to you gaining a deep understanding of the fundamentals of Moon magic and its many manifestations through reading this book. We will discuss how the moon's phases affect magic, how to utilize lunar magic in everyday living, how the Moon corresponds with the Triple Goddess, what special moons are, and tools you'll need for Moon magic. I have provided you with several rituals and spells for you to perform for each phase of the moon, and so much more. Even if you are new to Moon magic, this book will give you all of the necessary background, traditions, and tools you need to start practicing lunar magic right now.

1

MOON MAGIC ESSENTIALS

I have been practicing moon magic to clear away negativity and to manifest my intentions for more than a decade. I often use the full Moon and new Moon when I am self-reflecting on what areas in my life I want to change, and what I want to experience more of. Moon veneration, worship, adoration, Moon deities, and symbolic representation of the Moon have been connected with the vibrational energies of the Universe and the rhythms of life. The sacredness of the moon—and the widespread phenomenon with which it is associated—has appeared in various cultures and eras throughout documented history. It is richly engrained in mythology and symbolism.

Lunar magic is seen in terms of the vibrational energy of the cosmos and is thought to govern the processes of all change vital to life. The cycles of the Moon's appearance and disappearance is the foundation for the widely known connection between the Moon and the land of the dead, the region souls travel to after death, and the power to be reborn. Likewise, the Moon's governance over the cycle of life associates the moon with fate.

MOTHER MOON AND HER POWER AND SYMBOLISM

The lunar phases represent immortality, eternity, and the dark side or enlightenment of Mother Nature. The Moon is a reflection of humankind's inner wisdom or the phases of human life on earth. As previously mentioned, the moon controls the season, tides, rains, and waters. It falls somewhere between the light of the day and the darkness of the night, and therefore is associated with the realm between the unconscious and the conscious. In astrology, the moon symbolizes the soul; in horoscopes, it mandates the person's ability for adaptation and reflection. It gives an analogy of the developmental stages of human life: infancy corresponds with the new moon, adolescence with the crescent moon, maturity with the full moon, and sleep or life's decline with the waning moon. Just the sight of the moon in the night's sky practically forces us to take pause and stand in awe.

Watching the moon during the night is mesmerizing, and when it is full, we are charmed by its grandiosity. It takes some effort to pause and notice when the Moon is barely visible, and we tend to forget about it until we learn that every shape and form it takes has meaning. One really interesting correspondence with the full Moon is the specific names it's given according to the month it falls on. It is important to cultivate an intimate relationship with Mother Moon, especially for witches. The more you know her, the more cosmic energy you can harness. For instance, every full moon has a name, but occasionally there are more than twelve full moons in a year. For instance, the full moon in August is called the Sturgeon Moon because it is the best time of the year to catch sturgeon fish, and a second full Moon in August is called the Red Moon because it appears reddish due to the light fighting its way through the Summer horizon.

Different cultures have given names to full Moons across the lunar calendar. Many of the Moon's nicknames have come to us from Native American culture because of their lifestyle, the cycles of the lunar phases were just as important a method of timekeeping as the longer solar cycle of the year, from which the modern method is derived.

The cycle repeats itself, symbolizing the Earth's natural processes and life's natural cycles happening with us and to us. The Moon dictates what happens on Earth, including our emotions and the ocean's tides. It affects animal behavior as well as human behavior, which is why—even in its most subtle form—it is a powerful symbol of influence. The phases of the Moon don't quite line up with the modern-day calendar or Gregorian calendar. Every so often, there is more than one full Moon in a month, and the second Moon is called a blue moon or a red moon.

Symbols of the Moon also include:

- Mystery
- Transition
- Renewal
- Rebirth
- Darkness
- Emotion
- Time

The Moon Represents:

1. The Natural Cycle

The Moon is constantly changing depending on where it is situated relative to the Sun and the Earth, which is why it's more visible some nights than others. Everything in life, just like the Moon, has its own cycle. It's like how people wake up every morning, go to school or work, come home, make dinner, watch TV, read a book, take a shower, go to bed, and get up the next morning to repeat the cycle. This ongoing cycle is what keeps us ticking.

The Moon phases also represent growth and decline. We start out young and full of energy, and then we reach our apex, symbolized by the full Moon's brightness. As we age, our energy levels drop, and our strength lessens like the cycle of the moon.

2. Femininity

The Moon is associated with feminine energy and, with the Sun, can be seen in the symbol yin and yang. Usually, the moon is connected to feminine characteristics, such as delicacy and passion. The yin and yang display the characteristics of the polarity of the Sun and Moon. The Moon is darker and cold; the Sun is bright and hot. They portray polar opposites, which is why the Moon corresponds with yin and the Sun with yang.

The Moon's cycle is around 28 days, the same as a woman's menstrual cycle. This is one of the reasons that the moon was considered female to the ancient people because it had a cycle like that of a female. For the Hellenic polytheists and the Wiccans, the Moon Mother is gentle, beautiful, kind, and nurturing. The full Moon symbolized the big round pregnant belly.

The Moon goddess, Changi, has been worshiped since ancient times by followers of the traditional Chinese religions. Changi bore twelve moons, while Xihe, one of her husband's other wives, bore ten suns. These two lunar goddesses, together symbolize yin and yang, as well as the Chinese lunar and solar calendars.

3. Subconscious

While sleeping, humans don't exactly know what is going on around them. The night is always full of mysteries and secrets, which connect to us without our knowledge, specifically to our subconscious dreams and thoughts. The Moon is behind the scenes, doing its job while we sleep. The phase of the moon directly affects our moods as it controls much of our fluid fluctuations. After all, almost three-fourths of our brain is made up of water.

4. Influence

Without our knowledge, the Moon influences our behaviors. For instance, a full moon can bring about overly emotional or irritated feelings, or a sudden sense of increased energy. For others, the full Moon can bring about angry and sleeping feelings. Some animals become much more active during a full Moon. It affects all things, because if one thing is influenced, there is a change that ripples through all things. This is known as the butterfly effect.

As such, the moon has an effect on us and everything around us, making it a powerful yet somewhat hidden influence on planet Earth.

5. Darkness

Since the moon is present at night time, it symbolizes darkness in a way that connects us to the darkness. The less full the Moon is, the darker it is. But, even when it is full, it is still dark outside. For many, this is a peaceful serenity, and for others, it is scary. Also, without thinking, we see the Moon as darkness because we compare it to the Sun. Witches are often comfortable on the darker side of this duality, but with all things balance is key. The Moon can also be associated with the darker side of our personality; the part of us that stays hidden, and like the moon, tends to reveal itself at night.

6. Mystery

The Moon and the stars carry a mysterious element. In ancient times, up until only about fifty years ago, the Moon was unexplored, even though it seemed so very close to us. It wasn't until Galileo, in 1609, did humans start to take more of an interest in the Moon as an entity. It wasn't until then did humans know, by way of the telescope, that the Moon has valleys, mountains, and other characteristics similar to the Earth.

7. Emotion

The Moon is often thought of as what governs human emotions, and that people are deeply affected by the size of the Moon. When full, it brings about strong emotions, as previously mentioned is obvious by its effects on animals.

- *Full Moon*: When the Moon is intense, like when it is full, anxiety levels can rise, and people can even feel a bit manic. The full Moon has also been documented to intensify nightmares and dreams, which can have an impact on the following day's emotions (Fellizar & Kahn, 2021).

- *New Moon*: When there is a new moon, people tend to self-examine or delve into natural introspection. We can't see the moon when it is new, so its available energy levels are lower. People tend to report feeling more fatigued, causing them to naturally turn to their inner thoughts. Witches can take full advantage of the new Moon's cosmic energy to set their intentions and figure out what they want out of life. The new Moon starts a fresh lunar cycle, so its energy naturally supports new beginnings (Kahn, 2020). The first half of the lunar cycle is a time for setting intentions and goals for spell crafting. Witchcraft during the first half of the lunar cycle is a good idea because as the moon grows—known as waxing—so do motivations and energies. This is a time to take on new projects, during this two-week period where the new moon is developing into a full moon.
- *Waxing Moon*: During the waxing moon, sleep disturbances can occur, which makes sense because as the moon grows, there is an increased energy because we can see and do more. Several studies on the subject indicate that sleep is significantly affected by the waxing phase of the Moon (Cajochen, et al., 2013).
- *Waning Moon*: This is the phase where the Moon's illuminated section is decreasing, slowing us down and giving us a sense of letting go, cleansing, and releasing. This is a good time to let go of any resentments and regrets. It's a time for forgiveness and purging what no longer has a purpose. It is time to donate your old clothes, throw away old

makeup, and to get rid of anything weighing you down. Refresh your altar, sweep your doorways, and prepare for upcoming magic.

8. Renewal

Each night we renew ourselves by sleeping, which is also the time when the Moon shines. Also, the Moon symbolizes the soul's renewal through reincarnation. Humans are born, grow into mature adults, continue to age, then eventually die, and the children's birth starts the cycle all over again. The concept of renewal or rebirth can be found in almost every religion or belief system and has been around since ancient mythology. Pagan religions, including Wicca, do not have such a direct concept of rebirth but instead believe in nature's elements, such as the Moon, Sun, water, and trees, which are continuously reborn and regenerated. For Wiccans and pagans alike, the rebirth symbols are also associated with mental, physical, and spiritual renewal.

9. Eternity

The Moon has been always there, even before humans gazed upon it. It is always somewhere out on the horizon. Because it always has been and always will be; it remains a symbol of immortality and eternity.

ASSOCIATION OF DEITIES WITH THE POWER AND ENERGY OF THE MOON

For millennia, humans have gazed up at the Moon and wondered about its association with deities and its divine significance. Most cultures throughout history have had gods and goddesses associated with the energy and powers of the Moon. In Wiccan and pagan rituals, lunar deities can be called upon for assistance.

Common Deities Across Various Cultures

1. Alignak/Igaluk (Inuit): For the ancient Inuit peoples, Alignak is both the Moon god and the weather god. He governs eclipses and earthquakes and controls the tides. Legend has it that he is responsible for carrying the souls of the dead back to Earth for rebirth. He is the protector of fishermen from the wrath of the sea goddess, Sedna. It is said that Alignak committed incest with his sister and was banned from the Earth. His sister, Malina, became the Sun goddess and Alignak the Moon god. It is said that the two reunite during the solar eclipse.

2. Artemis (Greek): Artemis is the goddess of the hunt. She is the twin sister of Apollo, who is a Sun god. She is portrayed in artwork of the post-Classical period as always being beside a crescent moon. She is also the goddess of purity, nature, and childbirth. She was the daughter of Leto and Zeus and became the goddess of wild things and the wilderness. Artemis in her Roman form is Diana. She is queen of the Moon and brings forth good luck. If you can't find something, invoke the goddess Artemis, and she will help you find it. Artemis, the lunar goddess, can illuminate your life, your magic, and your spells.

3. Cerridwen (Celtic): In ancient Celtic legend, Cerridwen is the keeper of the cauldron that holds within it all knowledge. She is the giver of inspiration and wisdom. As a Moon goddess, she corresponds with intuitiveness. She is known by the full Moon and often represented as a white sow, symbolizing fertility, maternity, and fecundity. She is the Crone and the Mother.

4. *Chang'e* (Chinese): In ancient Chinese legend, Chang'e is the Moon goddess. She was married to a great archer, King Hou Ti. But he became tyrannical and spread destruction and death all over his land. He treated his people with brutality and starved them. He greatly feared dying and went to a healer who gave him a magic potion that allowed him to become immortal. But Chang'e stole his elixir while he lay sleeping, so he could not live forever, for that would have been a terrible thing. King Hou Yi went after Chang'e and demanded she give him back the potion. She drank it immediately and flew up into the sky, becoming the Moon. Chinese mythology cites this as an example of self-sacrifice for the best interest of others.

5. *Coyolxauhqui* (Aztec): Ancient Aztec folklore tells the story of Coyolxauhqui, the sister to Huitzilopochtli, an Aztec god. She was killed, along with all of her siblings, when her brother leaped from their mother's womb. Huitzilopochtli decapitated Coyolxauhqui and threw her head up into the sky, where it became the Moon. She is portrayed in Aztec artwork as beautiful young woman, adorned with lunar symbols and decorated with bells.

6. *Hecate* (Greek): The Dark Goddess, Hecate is associated with the dark moon, magic, and the spirit world. She is the goddess of ghosts. In ancient Greek poetry, when Hecate was born of Artemis and Apollo, Phoebe, a lunar goddess reappeared during the moon's darkest phase. Hecate banishes evil and is the goddess of the intersection of the three paths. Invoking Hecate helps bring things to an end. She is there for funeral ceremonies, remembrance, and rites of passage to the other world. She personifies the prophecy circle of the dark moon and should be invited when in need of great insight and wisdom. Perform a dark moon

ritual with Hecate for fresh starts and to gain ultimate feminine foresight.

7. *Selene* (Greek): Selene is a herald in Greek mythology, as she was praised and worshiped during the full moon. She had a young lover, a shepherd named Prince Endymion. Zeus granted him immortality; however his immortality was to be spent in a cave, sleeping forever. Out of her love for him, Selene came down every night from the sky to sleep next to him. Early classical Greek poets depict her as the moon incarnate. Selene cast light on to the Earth, and therefore on all living things, inside and out. She is the teacher of all things magic and supernatural through passing on her gifts of intelligence and special knowledge, granting those you invoke her the ability to have clarity.

8. *Hina/Sina* (Polynesian): One of the most well-known Polynesian lunar deities is Hina, or Sina, who lives within the moon itself. She is the protector of night travelers. According to ancient Hawwiian legend, Sina once lived on the Earth but grew tired of the way her family and husband treated her, so she packed up all of her things and went to live on the Moon. Tahitian folklore tells the story that Sina was curious and wanted to explore the Moon, so she paddled her magic canoe and flew to the Moon. Once she arrived, she fell in love with the Moon's tranquility and beauty and quickly decided she never wanted to leave. She is the oldest known goddess and is associated with feminine energy (wahine). Hina is known for her healing properties and is portrayed as Maui's wife, sister, mother, or grandmother. Hina watched over childbirth, and female babies were often dedicated to her.

9. *Thoth* (Egyptian): Ancient Egyptian lore holds Thoth to be the moon god of wisdom and magic. In some Egyptian

legends, Thoth is said to weigh the souls of the dead. In ancient Egyptian artwork, Thoth is portrayed with a crescent on his head. Invoking Thoth brings forth the workings of fate, wisdom, and magic. He is the one to involve when you write your Book of Shadows, a spell, or cast words of healing. You can also invoke Thoth to help you mediate a dispute. He was one of the most important Egyptian lunar deities and was said to be self-created, and therefore also became the god of equilibrium, corresponding to both chaos and order.

THE MOON AND THE TRIPLE GODDESS

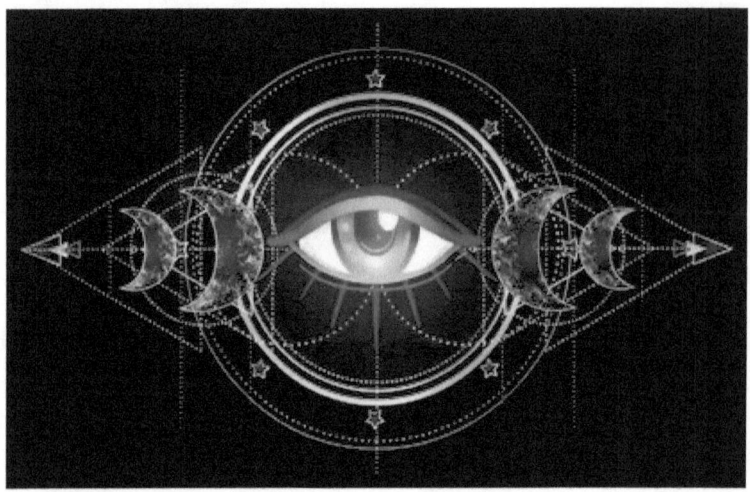

The Triple Goddess, who is revered in Neopagan religious and rituals, represents the trinity of the Maiden, the Mother, and the Crone—a three-fold form depicting the phases of female maturity and are also aligned with the Moon's phases as it orbits around the Earth. The waxing crescent, the full moon, and the waning crescent. But while all females move linearly through each of the phases during her lifetime, each of the Triple Goddess's aspects has characteristics that resonate in all of us, both female and male, at varying times in our lives. The Triple Goddess also reflects upon the complexities of the human mind—spiritual, mental, emotional—as well as the cycle of life that Earthlings experience.

Each of the Triple Goddess's aspects corresponds with specific seasons, the natural elements, human characteristics, and other naturalistic phenomena. These correspondences can be used to involve the most suitable aspect of the Triple Goddess for ritual ceremonies, spellcasting, prayer, and worship.

The Waxing Moon and the Maiden

The Maiden aspect of the Triple Goddess represents the youthful stage of a female's life and aligns with the crescent-to-waxing phase of the Moon. The waxing moon represents a period of growth, as it transforms into fullness. These phases of the Moon are reflected by the Maiden in the cycles of nature and correspond with the Spring season, dawn, and sunrise. The Maiden is also known as the Virgin or the Huntress. Her correspondence with Spring portrays her as innocent and young. When there is a waxing moon, invoking the Maiden or Persephone, Artemis, Rhiannon, or Freya works for any type of new beginning, such as new love, new employment, a new home, a new baby, etc. White is the symbolized color for the Maiden, who shows her face while the Moon is waxing. She is associated with innocence, independence, youth, self-confidence, self-discovery, exploration, intelligence, and creativity.

The Full Moon and the Mother

When the moon becomes full, the Maiden transforms to the Mother, giving birth to bountiful riches to all on Earth. She represents Summer and midday, the greenest time of the year with flowers and forests flourishing—and animals growing from youth to maturity. For humans, she is associated with adulthood, nurturing, responsibility, and the fullness that life has to offer. The Mother, as the full moon, is considered by witches to be the most powerful aspect of the Triple Goddess. The Mother Goddess was the inspiration for Gardnerian Wicca's understanding of the divine feminine. Invoking Demeter, Selene, Ceres, Danu, or Badb as the Mother Goddess in lunar magic is best for marriage, big decisions, fertility, and childbirth.

The Waning Moon and the Crone

The nights grow darker as the Moon wanes, and the Crone assumes her position of power. Also known as the Hag, she is associated with the later years of life, specifically post menopausal. She corresponds with Winter and Autumn, night, sunset, and the end of the growing season. She is the wisest aspect of the Triple Goddess, and governs past lives, aging, visions, death and rebirth, prophecy, transformations, and guidance. She was feared as an entity for thousands of years because she reminds us that death is a part of life, just as the dark phase of the Moon introduces the new moon. The Hag or Crone goddess is associated with the underworld and death. Invoking the dark Goddess Hecate, Baba Yaga, Morrigan, or Cailleach Bear should be used for magic, sorcery, ghosts, and the spirit world.

The aspects of the Triple Goddess are indeed a complex and diverse declaration of the divine feminine. For Wiccans and pagans who worship her, she provides constant opportunities to grow and learn through aligning with her three aspects. Making a conscious effort to align your adoration with the phases of the Moon will provide you with a more rewarding and an even deeper spiritual connection with the Triple Goddess.

CREATIVE PULL AND INFLUENCE OF THE MOON

Traditional Wiccan approaches to rituals and magic respect the principles of sympathetic magic. Sympathetic magic dictates the timing of ceremonial magic, and rituals should align with the energetic shifts of the Earth when possible. The influence of the Moon's cosmic energies cannot be denied, as we continuously bear witness to its creative pull in the changing tides, our behavior, subconscious or dreams, and the cycles of the human body. Synchronizing our lives with the Moon's phases can help us live in greater harmony with nature, its elements, and its ever-changing seasons.

Mother Moon is the celestial neighbor that lives closest to us. Even though in size, it is much smaller than our other celestial friend, the Sun. When it comes to gravitational pull, our Moon, be it a small satellite, expends two and a half times the gravitational force of the sun (Dragonsong, 2021). The Moon governs five tides, each of which are vital in the Earth's capabilities of supporting life. To Wiccans and other pagan religions, the Moon corresponds to the female facet of divinity and embodies the characteristics of Yin—which include fluidity, eternity, ever-changing, and life-bearing. Mother moon provides a soft light that guides us through life's many mysteries.

The creative influence of the Moon and the important aspects of life she affects include five primary Wiccan paradoxes and processes:

1. Chaos and Mystery
2. Evolutionary flow
3. Birth & Death
4. Soul and Emotions
5. Magic and Wisdom

The documented influences of the Full Moon include:

- Triggers breeding cycles and life's natural rhythms.
- Marks ovulation periods in humans and herbivores.
- Peak deer mating season happens during two full moons.
- Annually, the water temperature and cues from the lunar cycle encourage whole coral reef colonies to release their sperm and tiny eggs (gametes) into the ocean. It appears as a beautiful underwater blizzard of cascading colorful flakes by the billions in orange, yellow, red, and white.
- Birds appear to migrate by following the Moon's patterns to find their path of migration.
- During the Hunter's Moon, also known as the blood moon, game birds return to specific locations, usually in the month of October.
- During the full moon, salmon and bears move. Also called the Full Moon Salmon Mover, which lures the bears to feed, thus putting them on the move.
- More animal injuries are reported during a full moon. Studies documented a 28 percent increase in dog visits to the veterinarian emergency room and a 23 percent increase in cat visits (Poppick, 2013).
- Studies indicated that oysters have a lunar rhythm for when they open their shells to spawn and eat. They tend to be significantly more closed during a full moon, and tend to spawn and eat during new moons (Daley, 2019).
- There is a 15 percent rise in automobile accidents due to the Werewolf Effect (McDermott, 2019). McDermott and his colleagues (2019) theorized

that the moon's intensity tends to excite drivers, and they become more easily distracted after a study of 850,000 accidents.
- Electrical charges in all living cells are amplified by the full moon (Andrews, 2018).

THE SYMBOLISM OF THE MOON PHASES

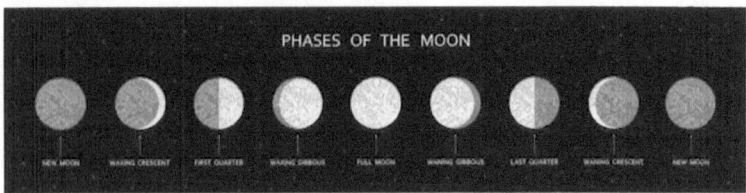

The phases of the Moon are so influential they can even be seen among the most popular tattoo designs. The Moon signifies spirituality and provides us with a feeling of connectedness to all that is cosmic energy. The Moon phases are just like a seed that grows into a seedling, then blossoms into a flower, and then dies. Once you learn to align yourself with the Moon, you can activate her natural powers and draw into yourself her innate characteristics of creativity, change, femininity, and fluidity. Male witches need to learn how to harness the powers of femininity just as much as female witches.

NEW MOON

The beginning of the lunar phases is dark and represents fresh beginnings or turning over a new leaf. It's time to pick ourselves up, set goals for the future, and plan for achievement over the next moon phase. Once a month, a new Moon happens when it conjoins in the sky with the sun. We can't see a new moon at first, but then it appears slowly, first as a very thin, illuminated crescent. Even though it is thought to last for three days, a new moon is only new for a moment, when the Moon and the Sun are in direct alignment in the sky. The new moon signifies the beginning of a cycle and can be thought of as a cosmic energy reset. It is prime time for goal setting and developing your intentions to manifest as the moon waxes into fullness. Aligning with the Moon's energies can help to give you a good sense of direction and grounding.

NEW MOON: MAGICAL PRACTICES FOR A NEW MOON:

1. Set an intention that is worthwhile. Each month the new moon offers up some extra intention-setting magic, so focus on those things you are specifically passionate about. Make sure your intentions are clear, specific, and concise as you can make them. You want to let the universe know your goals and aspirations during your New Moon Ritual.
2. Have a candle lighting ceremony. It is the darkest night of the whole month, so candles burn bright. Ask the Moon to illuminate you during this phase and all the phases to follow. Make sure your candle is charged and in a safe spot to burn through the night.

3. Start something new. The Moon is most fertile when it is new. Apply for that job you have been wanting, learn a new language, most of all do something novel.
4. Write a new moon wish list. Write down the details of your wishes. If you wish for new furniture, describe its color, shape, and size. Picture an image of your wants and focus on what it means to you.
5. Create a sacred moon altar for holding your moon-blessed objects and water.

What to Avoid During a New Moon

1. Quitting a situation or leaving person you care about. Use your energy to start something new rather than end something.
2. Not meeting new people. Don't miss out on the lessons and possibilities of new friendships or love interests.
3. Declining invitations. Get up and go, a new moon is the perfect time for accepting random invitations to anything,
4. Spending time with exhausting people—energy suckers.

CRESCENT MOON

The crescent moon represents femininity, growth, and thriving. Many years ago, it was thought to be symbolic of acquisition or conquest, but witch-hunters considered it to be a threat, so they would light a symbolic representation on fire in the land where a witch lived to let them know they were marked. The crescent moon is considered sacred to Wiccans, as it is associated with feminine power, psychic visions, the divine feminine, and creation.

Crescent Moon

WANING CRESCENT MOON

When the crescent moon is waning, its magic is used to banish negative or evil energies that are within a situation or a person. It is also worshiped when its magic is needed to remove hexes, end a relationship, break a spell, and help us to remember important things while starting on a fresh beginning. When the crescent moon is waning, it is referring to endings, doors closing, relationships ending, and previously casted spells ending. It is sometimes showing you to let go of something you no longer need but are still trying to hold onto. Use waning crescent moon magic for closing the doors on bad health, bad luck, and bad relationships! It symbolizes lessening—a lesser or lower state of movement and power. It is a time to compartmentalize and give in to feelings of sadness so you can let it go. The waning crescent moon represents the passing of time.

Waning Crescent Moon

Magic Acts for the Waning Crescent Moon:

- Removing negativity
- Breaking hexes and curses
- Cleansing objects and other people
- Cleansing rituals for your home and yourself

- Ending a love spell that has been placed on you
- Ridding yourself of negative personality characteristics and bad habits (addictions, etc.)
- Ridding yourself of your enemies once and for all
- Releasing pent up anger or rage
- Clearing the clutter from your mind

WAXING CRESCENT MOON

When the crescent moon is waxing, it symbolizes those new beginnings, gearing you up for the start of new projects or when you want to bring new things into your life. As the Moon heads toward fullness, your energy level will increase, providing you with the strength you need to complete your projects. It is a time to plan for the future, make wishes, and realize your hopes. It is a time to declare our desires for the new lunar month and hope for the best.

Waxing Crescent Moon

Intention Spell for Waxing Crescent Moon

1. On the first day of the waxing crescent moon, go outside.
2. Write your intention with a sharpie on a bay leaf and hold it between your palms.
3. Express your gratitude to the waxing crescent moon for coming to your ritual by holding your hands toward the moon and saying thank you aloud.
4. When you start feeling the vibrational energy of the waxing crescent moon, pull your hands with the bay leaf toward your heart.

5. Meditate on your intention and visualize it as if it has already manifested.
6. Light your bay leaf on fire and let it burn completely in an abalone shell.
7. Watch the smoke and ashes of the bay leaf float up toward the moon.
8. Trust that your intention was received by the Moon and know it has already started to manifest.
9. Thank the moon and complete your spell.

FIRST QUARTER MOON

The first quarter moon represents the importance of having a head start for facing and conquering the challenges you were not prepared for, it is also the symbol for the time to make impulsive decisions and act. It is the best time for conducting magic to draw things in, such as money, love, success, good health, and a productive time for calling back lost objects. The first quarter moon is a time to acknowledge any obstacles in your way, keeping you from getting your needs met. It is a time to focus on unblocking and aligning your chakras, taking spiritual baths, lighting candles, and maybe trying some nature-oriented exercise. The first quarter moon magic is great for success, abundance, and love. It is time for hard work and action with the arrival of the first quarter moon. It is a time to be prepared and flexible to make important decisions when things don't go as planned. Try a new recipe or cast your favorite attraction spell. The best time to cast a love spell is during the first quarter moon, and if you can do it on a Friday and a first quarter moon, it will have double the manifesting power. Remember, Friday is Venus Day.

FRANK BAWDOE

First Quarter Moon

GIBBOUS MOON

Waning Gibbous Moon

Waxing Gibbous Moon

Waning Gibbous Moon

The waning gibbous moon phase is between the full moon phase and the previous quarter moon phase. The word waning means diminishing. It looks not quite full, but a bit more than half illuminated. It rises later in the night than the full moon. You can usually see it in the early morning hours, and it is quite spiritual. Sometimes, you can catch an eerie glimpse of it looking like a misshapen, glowing red moon when it is close to the horizon. This is an important time to think about what you have pent up and need to release. Consider anything blocking you from achieving your desired outcomes. Your energy levels may be slowing down, but also leaving you feeling satiated and grateful. To make the most of this phase of the Moon, make a gratitude journal and use it for all of the phases. This is a perfect phase of the Moon for sharing the love, taking a friend out for lunch, reconnecting with old friends, and apologizing to anyone you snapped at during a full moon.

Waxing Gibbous Moon

The waxing gibbous moon is much like the waxing crescent moon, but when the gibbous moon is waxing, the illuminated section of the Moon is increasing, to eventually become a full moon. During the waxing gibbous moon phase, you can be facing some challenges. It is a good time to practice patience. Do your best to stay flexible and take a moment to jot down things you are grateful for. Pay close attention to your inner-being and trust in yourself. The waxing gibbous moon phase is an opportune time for consulting the Runes or Tarot cards. It is the time for evaluation, taking a step back, and looking closely at your life. What are we doing right? What are we doing wrong? If you want answers to those questions, simply ask the waxing gibbous moon! Correct your actions if needed and adapt to your current situation. During the waxing gibbous moon phase, it is a good time to improve and refine the intentions you set during the new moon.

FULL MOON

The beautiful, big, and bright full moon is the most iconic, notorious, and spectacular moment of the lunar cycle. The full moon is both figuratively and literally a time of illumination and culmination that can help us realize the fruits of our labor, bring energy levels to a head, and see things with more clarity. Often associated with howling wolves, intensity, and chaos, the full moon has earned its reputation. Because the full moon is the biggest and brightest moment of the lunar cycle, it brings energy that is just as extreme. Full moons can turn the quietest of individuals into social butterflies, but take caution not to wear yourself out. The full moon is quite literally your cosmic guidance counselor.

In the full moon phase, the Moon, Sun, and the Earth are in perfect alignment. Differing from the new moon phase, the full moon is on the opposite side of the Earth, so we see the side that the Sun is shining on. The Moon and the Sun are opposing signs on the zodiac, so you may feel some frustration and a bit of tension as the opposing energies are pulling on you. To make the most of the full moon phase, embrace your added energy and channel it into activities and projects you feel passionate about. This is the time to realize and manifest the intentions you set for your magic during the other phases of the Moon. It is the time for the completion of objectives you set and reach the peak of your prowess! It is also a symbol of power and purity. The full moon is a master charger, so set your vases, cauldrons, kettles, and anything else that can hold water outside under the full moon. I put mine on top of my car at nightfall and bring it in at dawn. I used the moon-blessed water for drinking, putting into my pet's bowl, watering my plants, infusing essential oils, added to my bath, anointing candles, charging my crystals, you name it, Moon-blessed water is capable of powerful magic.

Full Moon

When the Moon was in its new phase, it was a good time for goal setting and starting new projects, but full moons are more about putting things into motion and finishing those projects. The full moon is also associated with shedding or releasing any toxic patterns or habits in your life.

Full Moon Ritual

1. Ground yourself: Find a comfortable place to sit and commune with the full moon. Ask Mother Moon to help you be present in the moment with her there to ground you.
2. Tune into Mother Moon and Mother Nature: Surrounding yourself with nature has a grounding and calming effect. Charging up your call to nature during a full moon can help to quell your anxiety and bring clarity to any unanswered questions. Being one with the full moon and nature is healing and will align your body with its natural rhythms. Take a nature walk or bathe in the forest.
3. Mediate with Mother Moon
4. Journal under the full moonlight: Even if you are just writing a description of how the Moon is making you feel.
5. Write your spells and charge them with the full moon. Leave your Book of Shadows on a table or rooftop under a full moon. You may want to put it in a waterproof bag—unless you are positive it won't rain.
6. Perform a Release Ritual: Write down the things that need letting go. Light the paper on fire and place it in a fireproof container. Watch the ash and smoke take your troubles away into the arms of the full moon.

FRANK BAWDOE

DISSEMINATING MOON

The disseminating moon phase is demonstrative and receptive. It is associated with transformation, communication, and the sharing of resources. It is the time in the lunar cycle to progress toward advancing your goals by adjusting any action you took during the full moon phase that didn't lead exactly to the intended outcome. The questions to ask yourself during the disseminating moon phase are: Did my goals contribute to the welfare of others? Did my idealism turn toward self-righteous indignation? During this lunar phase, you will see a clear picture of the lessons you've learned through your life experiences and self-awareness. Teach others what you have learned. Make an offering to the moon by gathering feathers, leaves, branches, shells, and place them on a stone altar under the Moon or a tree stump as an altar. If they are not available, create a sacred circle on the ground and place your offering in the middle. Express your gratitude to Mother Moon for her love and support.

Disseminating Moon

The disseminating moon connects to the first quarter phase of the lunar cycle and the awareness of the movement or position of your body. It represents the challenge of aligning your personal vision with the needs of the collective. Move your body through sport or dance to unblock and align your chakras. Share your knowledge and visit old friends. Demonstrate your appreciation to Mother Moon by giving back to your community. be grateful for everything you have, all the special intentions you worked for, and acknowledge the importance of being hopeful for the future.

FRANK BAWDOE

LAST QUARTER MOON

The last quarter or third quarter moon phase is about spiritual healing and the advent of the time where you need to move forward, let go of past pain and feelings that caused you to hurt. The last quarter lunar phase is leading you toward redirection, accepting responsibility for your actions, transitioning, and completion. It is a time to draw on your inner strength to acknowledge any mistakes made and reward yourself for your successes. During this lunar phase, it's a time to get creative and be willing to take some risks. You may need to change some aspects of the foundation you have already built. You do this by figuring out what is working for you and what isn't working for you. Then take corrective action or make that final push toward successful completion. Then it is time to ask yourself, "Now what?"

Last Quarter Moon

The last quarter moon phase connects to your senses, touch, smell, and taste. Using your senses will help you successfully complete the cycle's goals. If your senses or your energy feels blocked, you can release it with tactile activities, such as seeing a chiropractor or a massage therapist, and through using your sense of smell with aromatherapy. The last quarter lunar phase symbolizes the end of the Moon's journey. For us, it means the last stage when you complete your work or when your efforts seeded under the new moon blossom.

BALSAMIC MOON

The balsamic moon is the final phase of the waning half of the lunar cycle before the new beginnings and fresh starts come along with the energy of the new moon. It symbolizes recovery and healing, time to yield and repose. It is a time to avoid taking actions that hurt you and to be still and at peace. This lunar phase encompasses the 3 Rs:

1. Rest: Get a good night's sleep and frequent rest periods during the day.

2. Rejuvenate: Plan a feel good activity, such as a massage or spend some alone time at the beach. Practice self-love.

3. Release: Let go of things that are not serving you. Visualize these things, write them down and burn them under the moon. Declutter your home, car, and office. Rid yourself of anything weighing you down so you can create new space for the fresh beginnings and energy that come with the new moon.

Balsamic Moon

SPECIAL MOON PHASES

When you take an interest in looking up at the night sky, chances are you will notice that the Moon never really looks the same as the night before. Even though a full moon means the face of the Moon is lit up completely by the Sun, not all full moons appear the same. Sometimes the Moon is glowing red, sometimes it looks huge. The Moon isn't actually changing size or color, it is where it is situated in relation to the Earth and Sun that affects its appearance to us. The following are some special moon phases, so you can set your magical intentions accordingly.

Blood Moon

Super Moon

Blue Moon

Harvest Moon

BLOOD MOON

Quite obviously, the reason why the blood moon is named so is that it glows red. A truly spectacular sight to see. I even set my alarm just in case I am sleeping to get up and spend some time with her. This special blood moon happens when there is a total lunar eclipse. The Earth is lined up between the Sun and the Moon, so the Moon is hidden from the sunlight. The only sunlight that reaches the surface of the Moon is from the outskirt of the Earth's atmosphere. The Earth's atmospheric air molecules scatter and block out the blue-colored light, leaving only the red reflection from the Sun, and the Moon glowing red. It is also called a blood moon when the smoke, haze, and dust in the sky make it appear reddish. Also, when the autumn leaves are turning red, the full moon is referred to as a blood moon.

During a blood moon, it is time to celebrate life, the blood running through your veins that is keeping you alive, and to make peace with your past. Use your spell crafting to increase your intuition and psychic abilities. The blood moon phase of the Moon is well suited for healing rituals and magic, specifically those pertaining to female issues, such as menstrual problems and reproductive health. Blood moon rituals invoking a deity or deities you feel closely connected to, or to perform other rituals designed to invoke the goddesses or gods of your tradition that are amplified during a blood moon.

SUPER MOON

A Super moon appears in the sky as a much larger-than-usual Moon. This is because it is closer to us. Astronomers refer to a super moon as a perigean full moon, which is a moon at its fullest and is at its closest orbital point around the Earth.

Super Moon: Supermoon Magic

1. Work with the element of water. Due to the exceptionally strong gravitational pull, the supermoon creates on the ocean tides, it is the perfect time to spellcraft with the element water.

- Springwater: Best for creativity, inspiration, and new beginnings spells.
- Rain Water: Best for garden magic, moon rituals, and house cleansing rituals.
- Ocean Water: Best for love spells, honoring or invoking sea deities, and power rituals.

2. Burn super moon incense anywhere in your home or on your altar.

- Combine equal parts dried lavender, cinnamon, and mugwort for the super moon. Burn it as a background to draw the super moon's energies or burn during a super moon ceremony.

3. Super Moon Cookie Recipe: Perfect for any witch, especially a kitchen witch. All you have to do is take your favorite cookie dough or cookie recipe and instead of making a batch of cookies, make one huge cookie. Just make sure it is thin enough not to be doughy in the middle. Offer to your family or your coven during the super moon.

4. Magnify the power of the super moon. Take a magnifying glass and charge your altar, objects, crystals, wands, you name it, and raise the power of the super moon by catching its light with your magnifying glass.

5. Perform a dedication or rededication. Ready to commit to a coven, deity, or a cause? Do so under the illumination of the super moon.

6. Drawing down the moon is an activity where you call a deity directly into your body. When conducted by a High Priestess or Priest, they are literally drawing the goddess into their body. Once the goddess is present, the Priestess or Priest is absent, and the goddess will speak directly through her daughter or son and interact with others at the ceremony. It is usually conducted at closed rituals with highly experienced members, as it is exhausting hard work, so if you are a newbie, give it some time.

7. Make super moon water. You can just place your water under the super moon overnight or you can use the following recipe:

8. Frank's Blessed by the Supermoon Water

You'll need:

- Super moon
- Clear quartz or moonstone crystal
- Lavender flower or drop of lavender essential oil
- Cinnamon stick or pinch of cinnamon
- Glass container
- Cauldron or pot
- Strainer
- Funnel
- Floating white candle

Directions:

1. Gather your ingredients
2. Boil the water and the herbs
3. Simmer for 30 minutes
4. Allow to cool and strain into your container(s)
5. Place your containers where you can see the super moon's reflection onto it
6. Put your crystal in the water.
7. Light your white floating candle
8. Thank the super moon, meditate, and put the candle out
9. Remove the candle wax the next morning.
10. Pour your super moon blessed water into a glass container or corked glass bottle.
11. Use for spellwork, charging items, drinking, etc.

BLUE MOON

We have all heard the phrase "nce in a blue moon." That phrase was actually documented as early as the year 1528. When there are two full moons in a lunar cycle, the second one is called a blue moon. A blue moon is much more powerful than a full moon and promotes powerful and significant spells. A blue moon only happens every 2 anf a half years. Spells and magic that happen during the blue moon often have long-term consequences, so remember that and don't use a spell when you are not sure about the effects. Meditation during this moon phase, as is divination, because of your heightened power is very important.

As I just mentioned, a blue moon is given to the second full moon that happens in the same month, but it was first given to any extra full moon that occurred in a season. Modern-day Wicca associates the blue moon with the growth of knowledge and wisdom. Pagan folklore provided names for moon phases to help people get ready for crop rotations and varying types of weather. The Moon has usually been connected to the mysteries, divine aspects, and intuition of the sacred feminine. In the Wiccan religion, it is sometimes associated with elderly women, and it is referred to as the grandmother aspect of the Triple Goddess. One thing is for sure, you can expect a boost in your magical workings during a blue moon. It is the perfect time for communicating with the spirit world and developing your psychic abilities. The blue moon inspires you to embrace your uniqueness and make any necessary tweaking to support your personal intentions.

Magical Practices for the Blue Moon

1. Take a spiritual blue moon cleansing bath using peppermint and chamomile. You can use essential oils, but for an extra special time use actual peppermint leaves and chamomile flowers.

2. Make a list of things weighing you down and that are no longer doing you any good and then burn it.

3. Meditated under the blue moon by connecting with its divine energy.

4. Write your intentions on a piece of paper and ask the blue moon out loud to manifest your desires.

5. Put on a blindfold, crank up the music, and dance.

6. Frank's Blue Moon Ritual

What you'll need:

- A candle
- Flowers, according to the season.
- A printed out image of the Empress tarot card.
- Sea salt
- Sage Incense, or you can smudge with a sage bundle.

Directions:

- Place all of your ingredients on your altar and chant these words out loud:

Empress of beauty, balance, and grace

Release my baggage, so I can pick up my pace

Drive them down deep into precious Mother Earth

So the next moon cycle, I can experience rebirth

So mote it be.

DARK MOON

The dark moon is actually a waning crescent moon that happens just before the new moon lunar phase. It is called dark because it doesn't reflect much light and is barely visible. Hence it is a time when many people will be feeling dark as well. It represents the dark aspects of the moon goddess pertaining to death and destructive magic. The dark moon is associated with stillness, introspection, soul searching, meditation, and dark magic. During the dark moon, go to bed early and get up late—radical rest is necessary. Spend some time consulting your runes, tarot, or oracle cards and tune into your intuition.

Dark Moon

Witchcraft you can do: hexes, curses, banishing, divorce, separation, and protection spells. This is a good time to meditate and perform divination rituals to get a glimpse into the future and see what awaits you. Cancel any plans you may have and spend time doing shadow work.

Shadow Work

1. Practice mindfulness

2. Invoke Hecate and ask her to please cast light on the shadow side of the challenges you are facing and to guide you through the struggles.

3. Create an altar especially for doing shadow work, a sacred space where you can explore the shadows.

4. Work with crystals that correspond with the dark moon, such as black obsidian, snowflake obsidian, rose quartz, and blue kyanite.

5. Paint, draw, journal, or write to tap into your shadow side. If you're feeling too positive, let yourself welcome those shadows that are within. It is a time for self-reflection. Once you become familiar with your shadows, you can communicate to the Universe or your deities what you want to work on.

LUNAR ECLIPSE

Since we know that the moon doesn't emit any of its own light, what we do see is the Sun's reflection off the moon's surface. When a lunar eclipse happens, the shadow of the Earth is blocking the Sun's rays, causing the Moon to darken temporarily. The good news is that everyone can see it, unlike a solar eclipse, which can only be seen by some.

TOTAL SUPERMOON LUNAR ECLIPSE

Some of today's witchcraft traditions feel that a lunar eclipse amplifies the power of your intentions, kind of like a cosmic bonus round. However, lately, there has been some discussion that practicing magic during the lunar eclipse is dangerous if you're a newbie witch. This is positively untrue. If you think that somehow your psyche can be damaged by the strength of lunar eclipse magic, please reconsider practicing magic at all. That type of thinking can self-sabotage your spell casting and ritual workings. I would recommend practicing your grounding techniques to safeguard against self-sabotage. Actually, lunar eclipse magic does wonders for spiritual development and personal growth rituals. The lunar eclipse is moon phase brimming with magic power. It happens once every year, and its magical powers are associated with change and symbolize major shifts in your life.

Lunar eclipse moon magic can include but is not limited to the following:

- Healing rituals or magic
- Drawing down the moon
- Drawing money
- Healing relationships
- Protection spells
- Spells to increase your psychic abilities
- Spells to raise your intuitive awareness
- Divination
- Asking Mother Moon for wisdom.
- Spells to boost your magical skill set.
- Rituals to honor lunar goddesses and gods.

FRANK BAWDOE

TOTAL LUNAR ECLIPSE

2

MOON SPELLCASTING: COMMON TOOLS AND PREPARATION

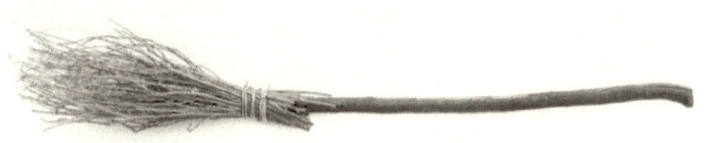

The only real required tool or ingredient for all magic is your intention. Any ingredient or object can become energetically and magically charged, so you don't have to buy the most expensive healing crystals or a $500 crystal ball. Cayenne pepper, cinnamon, sugar, and sage are powerful ingredients that can be used in a variety of infusions, oils, and potions. You can make just about any candle into a magically charged device. It is totally up to you, as long as you are confident in what it means to set your intention, cleanse your items, and make magic, you are good to go. After all, a cooking pot can become your cauldron, and a stick from the yard your wand. The magic is inside you.

MOON ALTARS

Similar to setting up any sacred altar, a moon altar is a magical place for you to harness and hone the various energies of the lunar cycle. A sacred moon altar is a place that you can focus, direct, and deliver your energy through your magical practice of witchcraft. You can perform meditations, rituals, and spells at your moon altar, or simply use it as a place of lunar worship. There is really no wrong way to set up your moon altar. It can be outside or inside, simple or elaborate, and anything in between. There are specific magical tools you can place on your altar that will definitely add focus and power to your moon magic, so get as innovative and creative as you want when setting up your moon altar, as long as it feels special, powerful, and sacred to you.

Types of Moon Altars

1. *Traveling Moon Altars*: You can carry your witchcraft tools with you anywhere you go. Simply take a drawstring bag and put some magical essence in it, such as a cinnamon stick or a few leaves from my favorite herb plant. Make sure to use travel-friendly tools in your bag, such as your runes, small gems, birthday candles, tarot cards, coins, colored ribbon. All of these tools are perfect for carrying with you to set up an altar somewhere in a natural setting under the moon.

2. *Stationary Moon Altar*: This is your usual altar set up in your home or office, only you are using magical tools specific for lunar rituals. I have a permanent altar set up in my dining room, near the patio, just to pay respect to every phase of the moon. The ideal aspect of a stationary altar is that you can deck them out with all different types of tools and trinkets without having to worry about damaging or losing any of your devices while traveling.

3. *Mental Altars*: Slightly less conventional, a mental altar may appeal to witches who are very good at and love visualizing. In your mind's eye, you can imagine your moon altar by picturing your sacred space, visualizing your tools, and placing it anywhere in the world you can imagine. A mental altar is a good form of lunar meditation, which goes perfectly with a lunar bath—bathing in the moonlight—or for divination rituals under the moon.

Altar Accessories

Along with candle holders for rituals to light candles, incense burners for spells require burning incense, crystals, and vases for flowers there are meanings behind each accessory.

Wands: direct energy, bless something, and consecrate sacred spaces or magical items

Frank's Wand

According to Gardnerian Wicca, the wand corresponds with the elements Air and Fire. I have a special wand for moon magic. It is oak and has a small, clear quartz on one tip that reminds me of the moon, and when I hold it up to certain moons, I can see its reflection glowing on the tip of the crystal. In Gerald Gardner's *Book of Shadows* (1950), he said his wand was "used to summon certain spirits." The same goes with my wand. I use it to summon the elements and the Moon. The element fire represents energy and power; hence the Wiccan wand is a magical tool used for directing your will and energy. Like the Moon, the witch's wand is strongly associated with magical transformation. Traditionally magic wands are used for many purposes in Wiccan rituals, and most are related to the direction or channeling of power and energy. Keep your wand on your moon altar and use it to cast your circle for your lunar rituals and to create your invisible, protective barrier around you when you practice your magic. Harness the vibrational energy of Mother Moon to direct its healing powers and to cast your spells.

Grimoire or Book of Shadows, you can use a notebook to document your lunar magical practices and spell work.

A Witch's Grimoire on Lunar Spells

Despite popular belief and things you see in the movies, there is not no single Wiccan Book of Shadows. Keeping a lunar grimoire is a perfect place to keep your moon spells, lunar correspondences and charts, invocations, ritual practices, a list of lunar magic rules, your favorite legends and myths, various pantheons, and anything else that can help you power up for the magic that comes with each phase of the Moon. Sometimes, a Lunar Book of Shadow's information can be passed along from one coven or Wiccan to another. Your lunar grimoire should be very personal to you. Once you have one, if you don't already have one, place it on your altar and perform this blessing ritual before and after your lunar spells:

In the Moon's magic realm, this book shall reside.

Only the Moon and the chosen can see what's inside.

Mother Moon protects it and shelters it from harm.

From moon phase to moon phase, it's blessed with her charm.

This grimoire is mine and contains no fears

My spells and my magic the moon goddess hears.

So mote it be

Crystals for Moon Magic

Crystals Corresponding with the Moon

There are various ways to use crystals in your moon magic and lunar rituals. Place a charged crystal corresponding with your intention in the center of your altar. I usually write my intention on a piece of paper and place it under the stone. In my humble opinion, I think that when you're working with different lunar phases, it is not so much about the particular crystal you pick to work with, because there are quite a few, but it is more about the intention you set for working with that specific lunar phase. In general, there are several gemstones that have vibrational frequencies that correspond with the moon, and it doesn't matter which lunar phase is occurring at that particular moment. The following are the crystals I recommend because their energies are specific to particular phases of the moon, but by no means are these the only crystals that work magic with the moon:

- *Selenite* is named after Selene, the Greek moon goddess. You can use it for amplifying moonlight, and moon energy, protection, and uplifting your mood. It is also great for charging and cleansing the other stones and tools you are working with.
- *Moonstone* is as ancient as the moon itself. When used for lunar magic, it can be used to guide and heal your inner journey, nourish your spirituality, and amp up your passion. With a waxing and waning moon, it has an esoteric, sensual feel as it evokes the peacefulness and tranquility of the moon. It releases a glowing surge of energy that can revitalize the body and mind and rinse away negativity. Moonstone crystals are enveloped by powerful rays of purple, blue, and gold and it is perpetually embraced by a glowing white energy making it a protective stone.
- *Labradorite* is a favorite crystal for any season or occasion, but it really shines when it comes to moon magic. It represents awareness, new beginnings, psychic powers, motivation for going after your heart's desires, and visioning. This gem, when utilized for a new moon ritual, embodies possibilities and potential for your future, but also enhances your visions, and fires up your inner spirit like the brilliant flashes of fiery color that sparkles from the darkness of the stone. It activates your senses and unblocks the third eye chakra.

Place it on your moon altar and let the stone guide your way through any struggles or challenges pointed in your direction.

- *Opal* is Australia's national gemstone and has been used in witchcraft since ancient times where it was known as a symbol of faithfulness and confidence. Opal was believed to have descended from the heavens onto Arabia as bolts of lightning. It was referred to as the *eye stone* during the middle ages, where it was used in magic to remedy poor eyesight. Use opal in your full moon rituals to summon the powers of the moon goddess. They can also be used to magically draw money from the moon.
- *Clear Quartz* is used in moon magic for its pure healing energy that supports the spirit, as well as the mind and body. Under a new moon, it draws away any discomfort or pain, and washes away negativity. It's a powerful amplifier and strongly enhances the moon's energies to their fullest potential.

Athames and other blades indicate directions and direct energies. Bladed tools represent masculine energy and the element air.

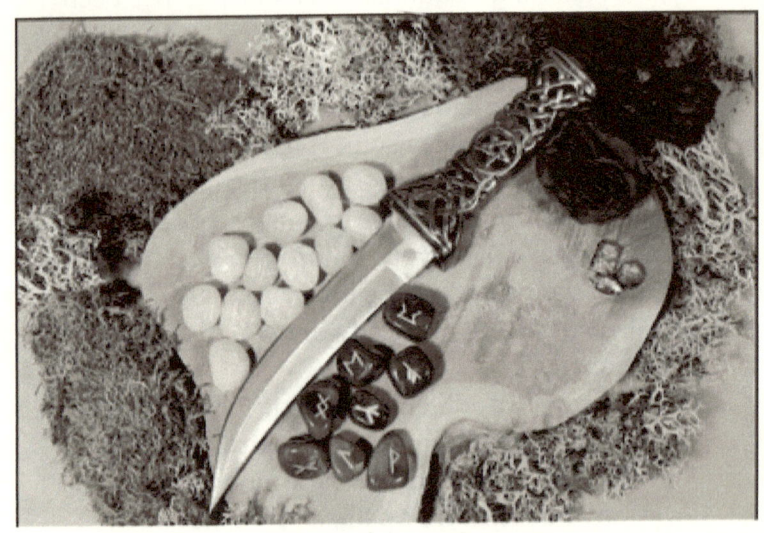

Lunar Altar with Athame

Athames are used in many pagan and Wiccan rituals as tools for circle casting and directing energy. It is a double-edged dagger that you can buy or have made by hand. The anthem is associated with air and fire, depending on your tradition. Pre-Wiccan traditions, such as the Hermetic Order of the Golden Dawn link it with the element air because its sharpness directs energy by moving it in the air, and sharpness is also connected to high intellect—as in sharp-minded. Because the dagger is forged in fire, many pagans believe it is connected to the element fire. For eclectic witches, you can just choose whichever makes sense to your intuition.

Chalice or goblet: a symbol of the goddess and her womb, it also symbolizes the element water.

Chalice preparing Moon Bless Water

The chalice, or goblet, is found in many pagan and Wiccan goddess-oriented traditions. Along with the cauldron, the chalice represents the womb and is considered feminine as a vessel in which life begins. The chalice corresponds with the element water and is perfect for preparing moon-blessed water recipes, such as the one in chapter one. I have a pewter chalice, but many of my friends have silver, ceramic, or wooden ones. I recommend keeping one on your lunar altar specifically for moon-based magic. If you are having a moon party, you can pass the chalice around and each participant can sip from the moon-blessed water. It will empower and bless anyone who drinks from it. It is a great moon-bonding activity where words like "may you never feel tired or thirsty" are spoken within a sacred circle under the Moon. Just make sure if you are drinking from your chalice that it is not made of any material containing lead.

Cauldrons are an essential tool for witchcraft and spell-making. It can be used to burn incense and herbs, brew potions, and perform water scrying to enhance vision.

Cauldron

Cauldrons are large pots, usually made of metal with a handle and a lid used to brew over an open fire. Dating back at least to the Bronze Age, the word *cauldron* is derived from old Germanic and Norse words meaning "hot place" (OtherWorldly.com, 2019). Back in time, there was no electricity, so the cauldron came as a great blessing for cooking and became associated with feminine magic or women's magic, and later witch's magic.

Magical Uses for Witch's Cauldron

- Cook moon food. There's nothing like making a cheese fondue to celebrate the moon being made of cheese. Sometimes, these somewhat silly stories that have been passed down through the generations are taken on as terms of endearment. It's a great way to celebrate a full moon with a belly full of cheese, especially if you have a Wiccan or pagan family. Children love dancing around a bonfire and dipping apples into the melted cheese in honor of a moon ritual.
- Brew concoctions and herbal remedies in honor of the moon gods or goddesses—or for healing purposes. Craft your concoctions and herbal remedies using healing, vibrational, and magical ingredients for your intended purpose. I create mine for clearing and healing, and you can too. Clear away things that aren't serving you. Making a full moon elixir is great for any lunar ritual and will intensify the magic even after the moon has set. You can make potions with your favorite herbs and some olive oil or coconut oil for topical use, or an elixir with basil, mint, cinnamon, and spring water. Just concoct it under the moon and leave in the moonlight for at least one night.
- Burn Incense
- Burn papers with written petitions on them.
- Burn offerings, such as plant matter.
- A safe place to leave a lit candle overnight.
- You can scrape the bottom and use the scraps to make black witch's salt.

- Use it as a symbol on your altar for the moon goddess or for the elements during your lunar ritual.
- Hold your moon collection aromatic potpourri.

MOON MAGIC WITH HERBS, FLOWERS, AND PLANTS

Altar Herbs

If you use plants, flowers, or herbs in your lunar rituals, you can arrange them in the shape of the moon phase under which you are crafting. I love to arrange a circle of dandelions on my altar when there is a full moon and jasmine in the shape of a crescent waxing or waning moon! Fresh herbs, plants, and flowers really make an incredible difference in the way I feel when I am performing a lunar ritual.

Another magical boost you can do with herbs, plants, and flowers is to represent the phase of the moon with the phase of the flower. Seeds and buds represent a new moon. Flowers just starting to bud for a waxing moon, and flowers in full bloom for a full moon. I take the petals of the flowers after they fall off or they're wilting and spread them around my moon altar to symbolize a waning moon.

Placing herbs, plants, and flowers on your moon altar symbolize Mother Earth and each of them has their own magical properties. In order for your lunar rituals to be successful, it's a good idea to pick up the herbs, plants, or flowers that match the moon's phase and your personal intentions. For instance, Sage and lavender are good for a lunar cleansing ritual, they both blow away negativity and help to purify limiting thoughts. For protection from Mother Moon, practice your lunar magic with mint and garlic. If you are asking Mother Moon for love, use coriander and cinnamon. If you are working on a project place violet on your altar as it corresponds with creativity. Ginger and dill on your moon altar make for successful business ventures, and to sharpen up your intuition—and for better sleep—adorn your moon altar with chamomile.

Boline: for cutting herbs

Boline

While there is no fast or hard rule as to what tool to use when cutting your herbs, Wicca tradition recommends using a boline as your magical cutting tool, for harvesting your herbs for lunar rituals. The best time to harvest them for your lunar altar is early in the day before the sun has a chance to dry them out. This way the herbs will keep their aroma and essential oils, which is an important instrument for moon magic. The oils are what maintains the fragrance. Cut and collect only the herbs you need that correspond with your intention for your lunar witchcraft. Certain herbs such as rosemary are best to snip off as an entire stem, but others, like basil, you can run your fingers down the stem and collect the leaves. Using your boline to manicure your plants will boost their magic. If you take a look at the image of a boline above, you will notice it is shaped like a crescent moon. If you are going to use your boline for flowers, such as lilacs or chamomile, wait until they are in full bloom to cut them. If you are performing a new moon ritual and using the seeds, make sure they are completely developed. I take a paper bag and place it over the head of my plants, such as on the dill plant, and shake it. The dry seeds easily come loose into the paper bag.

Compasses: helps you move in the right direction, harness the right energies, and help you to align yourself properly.

Witch's Compass

The magical circle is a part of the narrative and heritage of witchcraft. Historically, there are hundreds of examples of witches gathering in a circle to feast, work magic, dance, and yes, worship the Moon. The same applies to today's magical practices. Within the realm of traditional Wicca lies the concept of the witch's compass. It is a way to mark out or delineate the sacred working ground and separate it from unsacred space. I have heard Wiccans describe the compass as being a space between the Earth and the spirit world, for within the circle, witches can invoke many spirits, commune with divinity, and summon magical forces.

In some Wiccan traditions, the compass is made up of three rings surrounding a fixed center point. Each of the rings symbolizes a different stage in the life cycle. Therefore, they are designed as working from the outside moving inwards toward the center point as a symbolic pathway through the stages of life and into the spirit realm. You can make your own rings. The first is made of salt, symbolizing life. The second is made of wood ash symbolizing death and rebirth. The third ring is made of wine, salt, and water and represents the waterway we use to crossover to the spiritual realm.

Candlelight Represents Moonlight

Lunar Altar Candles

Since candlelight represents moonlight, you can use any kind of candle as a magical tool. I like to use white tea lights because they remind me of little moons. They make black ones, too for when there is a new moon. You can also make your own moon candles for divination or spells. Burning your intentions with your moon candle is a fantastic magical activity. Candle gazing and moon gazing at the same time is an incredibly powerful meditation. For a full moon and a waxing moon, light a candle, and leave it unlit during a new moon or a waning moon.

If you are using a new candle, place it on your moon altar and smudge it or light some incense around it to energetically cleanse it. This also creates a wonderful aroma for your moon ritual to come. Next, you'll want to infuse your intention into your candle for the upcoming lunar phase. What are your dreams and hopes for the next couple of weeks? How can you navigate this lunar cycle with authenticity and strength? Journal your thoughts on these types of questions. That's right, get writing! Try to come up with a single word that encompasses what you want to manifest with your lunar intention. Then, scribe your word, your initials, and a symbol onto your candle, or draw a tiny moon in the phase that you are going to be casting your spells. Candles summon deities, work your manifestations, represent the element fire in spells and rituals, and symbolize gods and goddesses in Wicca. Anoint your candle with olive oil or essential oils.

Burin: used to carve symbols into candles, wood, and other magical objects.

Burin

A burin is a sharp tool with a pointed end used for ceremonial magic and witchcraft for marking, carving, and scribing magical items such as your candles. Wiccan traditions engrave symbols and signs into their wooden wands, and the candles they used for lunar worship. Similar to the white-handled knife used by covens for many rituals, the burin can be used as a personal tool at home by witches, whereas the white-handled knife can only be used inside of a sacred circle during a ritual.

Wiccan White-Handled Knife

Broom or Besom: for cleaning dirt, negative energies, and removing bad influences before lunar magic and spell work.

Besom

An essential tool for your lunar rituals is the witch's besom or broom. We've all grown up with Halloween pictures of the witch flying on her broom across the front of the Moon, which is actually documented in art from the early fifteenth century (Gannon, 2013). The hallowed instruments of magic have been used since ancient times to sweep out negativity while sweeping in happiness and prosperity. Wiccans consider their besoms to be so powerful that filling it with intention makes it come true.

Bells and Rattles: used to summon spirits, get rid of dark energies. and evil presence. Rattles and singing bowls bring peace and harmony to a sacred space or cleanse a magical ritual.

Witch's Bells and Rattle

In paganism and Wicca, handbells have historically been used for ritual. The sound of vibrations given off by the ringing of bells has been believed to ward off evil spirits, and possess spiritual or magical powers for centuries. The sounds of the witch's bells represent creative power and are kindred with the divine. Keep them on your altar for use during lunar rituals to bring harmony and boost your powers. Dance with your bells under the moon to invoke the moon gods and goddesses. The sound of a rattle also causes vibrations that are a great source of power for communing with the moon goddess. In some Wiccan covens, a bell tolls 40 times to summon the dead the members one wishes to honor. You can use your anthem or any of your other magical tools to sound your bells and rattles.

Clothes: for lunar rituals. It can be a cloak, robe, or mask that will help you achieve the right mindset to perform the magic.

Ritual Robe

Something can be said for wearing lunar ritual robes or cloaks, as they have been worn by pagans and Wiccans for centuries as a way of separating themselves from an ordinary day and enhancing their sense of mystery and magic. Donning a cloak is as much a part of the spiritual and mental preparation for lunar ritual as it is to dress your lunar altar. Some witches prefer ritual robes for their moon magic practices. It is a personal choice, but many witches I know who practice Wiccan tradition, do not wear anything underneath. But a cloak usually only fastens at the neck, so you might not want to be naked. As always, do what makes you feel most comfortable.

Robes can be handmade or purchased. There are loads of patterns online that are simple to assemble if you're like me and not a very experienced sewer. You can wear any color cloak to match your lunar phase worship or your intuition. Both white and blue correspond with the Moon. But I have seen pink cloaks and bright yellow ones too. Make one hundred percent sure that you have non-flammable clothing on for any ritual, as candles and bonfires can lead to accidental problems, especially when there is a breeze. Most have hoods and sleeves, but if you live in a hot climate you can find them without.

Spears: popular witchcraft tools for Wiccans that represent the Horned God in rituals.

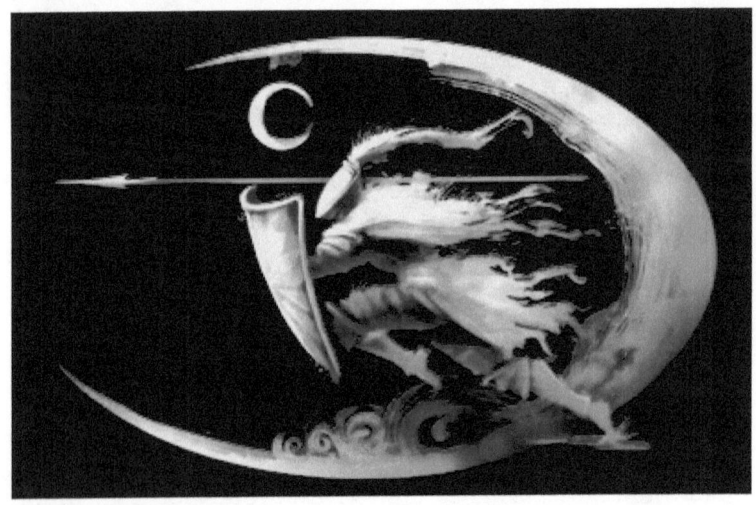

Witch's Spear

The spear is documented all the way back to 400,000 BC (Ingenito, 2021). It was used as a hunting tool and a weapon. You can make a symbolic small spear to place on your lunar altar to honor the Horned God and to focus your intention upon during a crescent moon ritual. Wiccan symbols such as a spear represent the Horned God and therefore correspond with a crescent moon phase. Your life experiences as a pagan or a Witch, your knowledge, and your present understanding of symbolic tools play a role in how you identify with each magical item on your lunar altar.

Offering Bowls: used for making offerings to the gods and goddesses.

Offering Bowl on Lunar Altar

For my lunar offerings, I collect stones, feathers, fallen leaves, a palm frond or two, sometimes on a new moon an egg, that I bury after the ritual. I do this for the days preceding the ritual and place it on my lunar altar. I surround my bowl with flower petals, candles, and crystals. I also put a nice crystal cup for my moon-blessed water to charge. All of the items will be charged during any lunar phase ritual. I know some witches who love to fill their offering bowls with delightful delectables, such as chocolate truffles, and other guilty pleasures made of cacao, in honor of the moon. Cacao translates to "the food of the gods and goddesses" in the ancient Aztec language.

Pen and Paper: an essential item to have on your lunar altar to pen down the intentions, dreams, desires, and emotions you want to get rid of, along with many other aspects of your magical desires.

Pen and Paper

Penning down your thoughts on a piece of paper is in itself a magical ritual. Learning how to draw sigils and symbols is a fascinating and spiritual process as well as an educational one. Drawing the phase of the moon you are about to perform in color for your ritual is part of focusing on the intention of your lunar magic. Drawing a hill with the moon setting upon it, or the moon shining through some tree branches, inspires your moon-given creativity and is enacting your artistic expression at the same time. It honors Mother Moon. Writing down your intention and its desired outcome is one of the best ways to clearly and specifically communicate what you want out of your lunar magic. It is like writing a note for Mother Moon to read herself. Another reason writing down your intention is a good idea is because by doing so you avoid an accidental manifestation of something you didn't want. For instance, if you are performing a money drawing lunar spell, you want to specifically ask for a large amount of money or you may end up winning a hundred dollar lottery ticket that will not help you out of a financial bind as I did.

FORMULA FOR WRITING OUT INTENTION

In the present tense, using the word *I*, write your specific desire + the time frame you want it to manifest. This is your intention.

For instance: "I drive a blue Ford Mustang to work every day" is more powerful than "I need a new car."

Intention Setting Lunar Ritual

1. Perform this ritual under the Moon on a blanket or sitting on the Earth, where you won't be disturbed.
2. Light three white candles and place them safely around you in a circle.
3. Make a ceremonial tea with a few drops of almond extract and some fresh mint, hopefully from your lunar garden.
4. Journal by penning down what your life looks like at the present moment. What type of relationship

you are in, how you spend your leisure time, in general how you are feeling.
5. Next, moon-gaze, focusing on how you want your life to be after you have manifested your intention.
6. Write down your intention following the formula above, filling in the gaps of what you wrote in what your life looks like now and what you wrote for how you want it to be after your manifested desire.

Pentacles and Pentagrams: represent the elements at each of its points, and are used for blessing items and tools, and charging objects, like crystals and chalices. Deeply ingrained in history, the pentagram is documented in artifacts from as far back as 3000 BC and was used in religious rituals by the ancient Greeks, and the ancient Babylonians. It is also documented in early Christian works for over five centuries as a symbol of the five wounds of Jesus Christ (Dual Crossroads.com., 2021).

Pentagram at Lunar Ritual

In Wiccan and pagan traditions, the pentagram symbol is not a representation of good versus evil. It is a symbol of the elements water, fire, earth, air, and spirit—with one point representing each element. The circle is symbolic of the Universe that holds and connects them all. The pentacle is a symbol of faith. One common misconception about the pentagram in Wicca is the direction in which it points. Pointing down does not mean toward the devil, and it should not be associated with Satanism. This misconception came about in 1966 due to the established Church of Satan, which endorsed the inverted pentagram encircling a goat's head as its symbol (Criger, 2021). In Wicca, the top point of the pentagram symbolizes the element air and corresponds with the spirit ascending above.

Lunar Calendars: detail the phases of the moon, help you prepare the spells rituals so that each spell will be cast at the right time in order for you to get the desired results.

Lunar Phase Calendar

As the Moon orbits the Earth—and the Earth orbits the Sun—over the course of the month we experience each of the Moon's phases. As the Moon takes its sweet time radiating, renewing, resetting, retreating, and resting every 29 days, so do we. We traverse different mindsets, ways of acting, and emotional experiences. We move or orbit around those experiences the same way the Moon moves or orbits the Earth. The more aligned we are with those phases and how they attune with us, the better able we are at harnessing moon magic. If you take into consideration each of the moon's phases and their particular energies, you have an opportunity to tailor your magical practices and witchcraft for each new phase of the moon. Keeping notes and keeping your eye on your lunar calendar is the best way to stay mindful of each lunar event. I hang mine just above my lunar altar.

PREPARING FOR MOON SPELLS

Preparing for lunar rituals around the Moon's energy has been a tradition across cultures of the world since ancient times. All around the Earth, all people are under the same moon, illuminating our evening skies to eventually become swallowed in darkness, only to miraculously start to grow again. Each lunar phase describes a different quality or energy, either receding or building, and specific rituals can be enacted to call upon those energies around each phase. Prepare yourself spiritually and mentally for your lunar spell castings, so you can achieve your desired outcome.

Whether you belong to a coven or you are a solitary witch, you can use your lunar calendar to pinpoint the moment the moon is new or full, so you can be as exact as you want to be for your ritual. The Moon represents your inner-being, and some of these traits you may keep safely hidden away from the rough exterior of the outside world. Vulnerability is an attribute associated with the Mother Moon or the moon priestesses. The Moon's element is water, corresponding to your emotional energies swelling and then receding like the tides. Deep feelings and sometimes sadness are expressed elementally in your emotions, and inturn, are welcomed in by the moon's circle.

Preparations

- Cleanse sacred spaces by smudging and lighting incense on your altar
- Choose the right time
- Find the right location
- Review the spell
- Prepare the tools
- Correct your state of mind. Focus your mind on the loyal companionship of the Moon. It never leaves you. It is always watching over you, steadfast, knowing your darkest moments, as well as your light. It changes just as you do, with every day being a different version of itself. Just like you, sometimes it is strong and bright; and sometimes just like you, it is waning and weak. The Moon reflects humanity, and all that it means to be human. What it means to feel alone and unsure, and cratered with imperfections.

RITUAL PRACTICES FOR EACH MOON PHASES

- New Moon - Set and reset intentions
- Waxing Crescent - Practice self-love and nurture your new ideas.
- First Quarter - Start action
- Waxing Gibbous - Refine and formulate your plans
- Full Moon - Illuminate and manifest your intentions
- Waning Gibbous - Reap the rewards of your lunar magic and express your gratitude to god and goddess.
- Last Quarter - Let go of things no longer serving you and release energy.
- Waning Crescent - Celebrate completing your cycle and get some much needed rest.

3

NEW MOON SPELLS

Did you know that you can use the lunar phases to manifest love, draw money, find a new job, and many other manifestations that come true because of new moon magic. Asking the Mother Moon to help you to start a new chapter in your life is best conducted during a new moon. It is the phase where rituals will help you to step into who you really are on a much deeper level. Understanding this phase of the Moon can provide you with success in your spell work, good fortune, and guidance from the goddess herself. It brings harmony, and makes you feel happier and energetic. The new moon phase is ideal for exacting, planning, and launching a business, it's great for money spells that will increase cash flow. Love spells are also a common practice during this lunar phase. Banishing spells, divination spells, and magic for fresh starts and new opportunities are all part of new moon rituals. Self-improvement spells—and curses—help you set goals during this stage of the Moon for the next upcoming cycle.

NEW MOON SPELLS, RITUALS, AND CEREMONIES

Start with decluttering to prepare for the ritual: light a candle, burn sage, turn on relaxing music, keep pen and sacred paper you to write, connect with divine energy source you relate with or other deities that represent the moon. When everything is set, sit down and relax. Write down the details you want for the future and explore your life. Finally, after declaring your wishes, sit quietly and meditate.

ATTRACTING A LOVER SPELL

This may seem like a very simple spell, but it is very useful and can be used for a variety of reasons that relate to attraction. Its intention is to attract your love interest to you; not only does it conjure up a lover, but it will bring you exactly what you ask for in a lover.

What You'll Need:

- New moon
- 4 red candles
- Pen and Paper
- 30 minutes of uninterrupted time
- Cinnamon essential oil

Directions:

1. Inscribe each red candle with a word, sigil, or symbol that represents your intentions.
2. Anoint your candles with cinnamon essential oil.
3. Set the marked candles in your sacred space side by side.
4. Write down your intention on a piece of paper. Be clear, concise, and focused.
5. Smudge your sacred space, and place your penned intention in between your arranged red candles.
6. Light all four candles, allowing the flame to settle into a balanced rhythm before carefully waving your intention over the flames of each red candle, consider using a pair of tongs for safety.
7. Let the fire completely burn your intentions, transmitting them to the lunar plane.
8. Be sure to practice caution when doing this, Use tongs or metal chopsticks to hold the paper and have a flameproof container to catch the ashes.
9. Take the ashes and throw them to the Moon while invoking the elements wind and fire to deliver your intention to the Mother Moon.
10. Place your candles in your cauldron and allow them to burn completely. Snuff them out if you do

not have a fireproof container, but remember to use a cleansed tool to do so.

NEW ROMANCE SPELL

It's a quick and easy new romance love spell that dates back centuries to when witches infused honey into love potions under a new moon. Spell casters use honey to bring a couple closer to each other with its natural sweetness. One can use it on crushes, exes, and disgruntled romantic partners. Moreover, consider the natural ingredient honey's stickiness to play a major role in gluing together a new romance

What You'll Need:

- A new moon
- A jar of honey
- A pen and paper

Directions:

1. Write your new lover's name three times on a piece of paper.

2. Rotate the paper 180 degrees, like the Moon rotates on its axis.

3. Write your name three times, overlapping the name of your new lover.

4. Focus on your intention on the new romance spell.

5. Write how you want your new romance to play out, in first person, present tense, and on the same paper as you and your new lover's names. Draw a circle around the two names representing the moon without lifting your pen.

6. Fold the paper gently and put it inside our honey jar.

7. Make sure to touch the honey with your fingers when you put the paper inside.

8. Chant this new romance incantation in a clear and loud voice:

> *My new honey is so sweet,*
>
> *(new lover's name) is sweet love to me.*
>
> *So mote it be*

9. Lick the honey off your fingers and then seal the jar with a lid or wax.

10. Rotate the jar in a circular motion symbolizing the moon before placing it on your lunar altar.

11. Thank the Mother Moon.

FACILITATING LOVE SPELL

This spell is best cast when the new moon is at its peak. However, if you can make it on that particular day, you can perform it one day before and one day after the new moon's maximum peak. To profoundly connect with this lunar phase, do this spell at night.

What You'll Need:

- New moon
- Red pen and paper
- Picture of your love interest
- One glass jar
- Petals of six dried roses

- Red piece of thread
- Three red candles

Directions:

1. Meditate and free yourself from all negativity and tension. Take your time.

2. Take a cleansing bath before you conduct this ritual.

3. Set up an outside moon altar and put your ingredients on it.

4. Smudge your altar and items.

5. Write your name and the name of the person with whom you are casting a facilitating love spell side by side.

6. Draw a red circle around both names.

7. Write on the back:

> *With these names and these petals,*
>
> *this new love will settle, in both of our hearts,*
>
> *we will never part.*
>
> *So mote it be.*

8. Roll the paper into a tube and tie the red string around it and then into a bow.

9. Place your scroll into the jar.

10. Make a triangle out of the red candles around the jar and light them.

11. Meditate on your love for 15 minutes.

12. Snuff out the candles.

13. Set the jar under the moon overnight.

14. In the morning, relight the candles.

15. Remove the scroll and use tongs to burn it.

16. Let the smoke and the ash take to the breeze.

17. Thank the Mother Moon for this new beginning.

FERTILITY SPELL

What You'll Need:

- New Moon
- One brown egg
- Blue and pink pen and paper
- Angelica essential oil
- Cinnamon essential oil
- Mint leaves (a handful)
- Blue candle and pink candle

Directions:

1. Make a nest out of your mint leaves on your lunar altar for the egg.

2. Draw an interlocking male and female symbol on a piece of paper and place it on your mint nest.

3. Massage essential oils into your egg.

4. Place your egg into its nest.

5. Light a candle on each side of the nest.

6. Cook the egg the next day and eat it.

I ask of you this night, oh special new moon

To enter fertility into the womb

With passion and loyalty the new moon's stealth

To bring forth a baby in perfect health

So mote it be

AUTHENTICITY SPELL

Resetting boundaries, pronouncing your freedom, setting your intentions, and releasing your most authentic self for the month ahead is exactly what is asked of the new moon each month.

What You'll Need:

- New moon
- Pen and paper
- White candle

Directions:

1. Create a new moon mantra and keep it simple. Here are some examples:

- *I am a visionary who sees wonderful things coming my way.*
- *I am intuitive*
- *I am filled with brilliant authentic expressions.*
- *I live a prosperous life: rich with compassion, friends, money, and love*
- *I am the light of my soul.*

- *I am infinitely creative*

2. Write it on the paper.

3. Place the paper on your lunar altar

4. Light the white candle for five minutes each day for until the next lunar cycle according to your lunar calendar. It will keep your mantra alive.

5. Speak your mantra every evening under the new moon until the next moon phase.

6. Concentrate on asking Mother Moon to help you to live your most authentic self.

JOB HUNTING SPELL

Hunting for a new job is much easier if you know how to align your intention and your energy with the vibrational energies of the new moon. Before you start this spell, spend a few moments determining the exact nature of the type of new job you want and the specific outcome you desire. Ask yourself, what are the benefits and salary you desire, what type of company you want to work for, and any other job concerns like the hours you prefer to work.

What You'll Need:

- New moon
- Pen
- Index card
- A green candle
- Honeysuckle essential oil
- Honeysuckle incense

Directions:

1. Light your incense and place it on your lunar altar. I have a small Aladdin's Lamp incense burner.
2. Write down on the index card the characteristics of the new job you want to attract.
3. Anoint the green candle with the honeysuckle essential oil, starting at the base and working up to the top using a clockwise motion.
4. Dab yourself in the center of your forehead, at the center of your heart, and on both temples with the oil.
5. In the evening under the new moon, hold the green candle with both hands, and visualize your intention and energy filling the candle. Focus on the pulsing and glowing acting like your beacon to the moon.
6. Place your candle on your lunar altar and light it.
7. Place the index card between your two hands and visualize already having your dream job. Picture yourself feeling excited, blessed, eager, motivated, and elated just as you will when you get the job. Speak aloud:

Mother Moon, call forth the right job for me,

I am excited to become a new worker bee.

Using my talents, my strengths, and my gifts

Good money, good hours, no longer a myth.

So mote it be

NEW MOON DIVINATION SPELL

What You'll Need:

- New moon
- Candle holder
- White candle
- One deck of oracle cards of your choosing

Note: In case you are unfamiliar with the difference between an oracle deck and a tarot deck, let me give a quick explanation. Like a deck of tarot, oracle decks are illustrated beautifully, with many different themes—lunar included. Both are created to be able to pull a certain sense or intuition from the deck to aid you in answering specific questions. Oracle cards do not need to be memorized or require any previous understanding. Each one of the cards has a message that is easy to understand and is clearly worded. Reading oracle cards requires no specific skill set. Oracle cards will provide you with guidance and affirmations about what you need to keep in the back of your mind moving forward.

Directions:

1. One the new moon has risen, place your candle in its holder on your altar and light it.
2. Perform some deep breathing exercises and center your thoughts on the goddess Selene.
3. Visualize a glowing white energy force moving up from the top of your head and connecting to the silvery glow of moon goddess Selene.
4. Sense and feel her radiant, cool light descending down from the Moon, even though it isn't visible,

and entering your body, filling you completely to the point of it overflowing and illuminating and surrounding your body, like a cocoon of shimmering moonlight.
5. Shuffle your oracle deck of cards.
6. Draw the top four cards and lay them down left to right.
7. The first card will guide you through the first week of the lunar cycle.
8. The second will guide you through the second week, and so on.
9. When you have completed your reading, express your gratitude to the goddess Selene.
10. Place your cards on your altar for review during each week of the lunar cycle.
11. Snuff out your candle.

ADVENTUROUS SPELL

What You'll Need:

- New moon
- Pen or pencil and paper
- Orange candle
- Orange essential oil
- Cinnamon powder
- Abalone shell
- Sage bundle

Directions:

1. Smudge your lunar altar with sage.

2. Draw a picture of the exact type of activity such as a sport, travel, hobby, sewing, ceramics, wine tasting, etc.

3. Place the picture on your lunar altar.

4. Focus your intention and mind on positive and healthy adventures—you don't want to summon a hurricane.

5. Anoint your candle with the orange essential oil.

6. Light the candle.

7. Speak aloud

> *Life is a blast and all is good*
>
> *Adventures to last*
>
> *Let's run in the woods,*
>
> *or make something new,*
>
> *or travel abroad.*
>
> *To endless adventures, Mother Moon gives a nod.*
>
> *So mote it be*

8. Sprinkle a pinch of cinnamon into the candle light.

9. Thank Mother Moon and wish her goodnight.

4

WAXING CRESCENT MOON SPELLS FOR TAKING ACTION

The waxing crescent moon comes about three to seven days after the new moon, and the main theme is manifestation. A waxing crescent moon is a good time to write down your objectives for the future and to focus and discipline yourself in manifesting your intentions. It is time for preparing for the next set of plans in preparation for the next lunar phase. Potential spells during this period focus on positive energy, attraction and protection magic, healing, wealth, success, friendship, luck, self-improvement, and inner beauty. The waxing crescent moon phase is a time for self-reflection and working toward your future goals and dreams.

BATHE ME IN CONFIDENCE SPELL

Bath magic uses elements like water, salt, and cleaning items—organic shampoos and lavender bath wash—in this ritual, run a bath, add epsom salts or sea salt, light a candle to set the mood, and prepare the environment. After that, take a bath, imagine all your intentions and goals manifesting, think of anything that can hold you back, and let those obstacles flow down the drain as you cleanse yourself physically, emotionally, and spiritually.

PASSION OVER THE MOON SPELL

A waxing crescent moon ignites the passions of sensual pleasure and love. Set the scene with your lunar altar dressed in red and pink items. Hang or post pictures of you and your lover, include a couple of magazine pictures with your favorite sexual positions represented. Setting a table with a dozen raw oysters in the half shell won't hurt either. Pour two glasses of burgundy wine, or fruit punch, and put on your favorite soft and sensual music.

What You'll Need:

- Waxing crescent moon
- One red candle
- Jasmine incense

- Wooden bowl
- Cinnamon candies
- 1 cup of rose petals

Directions:

1. Turn the lights down low and open the blinds or curtains if you're inside so you can see the Moon.

2. Put your cinnamon candies on your lunar altar inside the wooden bowl.

3. Stand before your lunar altar and line your rose petals across it while chanting

> *Oh Waxing Moon, with love's delight*
>
> *With this burning flame, let passions ignite.*

4. Light the red candle.

5. Light the jasmine incense and take in its aroma.

6. Spend a moment in the aroma, gazing at the candle, and building your feelings of passion.

7. Suck on some of the cinnamon candy, imagining it filling you with passion and joy.

8. Turn up the music and dance under the moon

FRANK BAWDOE

GRANT ME PATIENCE SPELL

What You'll Need:

- Waxing crescent moon
- Howlite crystal
- Six blue tea lights
- Paper
- Blue pen
- Sigil for patience. You can copy and draw the sigil here and and put it on your lunar altar for the spell.

Directions:

1. Cleanse your area for the lunar ritual, including your altar. Make sure all items are charged.

2. Draw your sigil. The sigil above symbolizes *patience*.

3. Write "patience" on a piece of paper or something like, "I am patient."

4. Put your howlite crystal on top of your sigil and written word(s).

5. Light the six blue tea lights around the sigil and crystal

6. Hold both hands together over the top of the howlite and say aloud.

> *My impatience has now come to an end*
>
> *My ability to wait and my attitude to bend*
>
> *I ask Mother Moon, for her patience to send*
>
> *I will calmly wait for her to attend*
>
> *So mote it be*

7. Bury your drawing and words on paper under the Waxing Crescent Moon.

8. Let your candles burn down or snuff them out to close the spell.

I MADE THE FIRST MOVE SPELL

If you are going to make the first move on a love interest, you first want to tell yourself out loud how you are absolutely desirable and a good catch. This spell is more powerful if you take the time to give yourself a makeover. Practicing a little self-love enhances any spell. Try changing your hairstyle, getting a new outfit, and generally inviting positive and new energies into your life.

What You'll Need:

- Waxing crescent moon
- A red tapered candle
- Tea tree incense
- Clear quartz crystal

Directions:

1. Smudge your space and charge your clear quartz crystal—smudging charges the crystal.

2. Light your tea tree incense to enhance your sexual energy for making that first move.

3. Point your crystal to the west for confidence and romantic desirability.

4. Place your red tapered candle in the center of your lunar altar and light it.

> *May I be seen as wonderful today*
>
> *Give me the confidence to make my way*
>
> *The reception is grand, I'm seen in good light*
>
> *Under the Moon, my first move's delight*
>
> *As it is and should be*

5. Visualize the crystal pulling the energy from the waxing crescent moon into your candle looping around, flowing through you, and shining bright.

6. Let the candle burn down, and thank the Mother Moon for responding to you.

7. Put the crystal in your pocket or purse and carry it with you when you make the first move.

8. Keep it with you until your desires are met.

CONFLICT RESOLUTION SPELL

What You'll Need:

- Waxing crescent moon
- Moon-blessed water
- Pen and paper
- 2 pink round candles
- A large enough mirror to place on your lunar altar and hold candles
- A picture of you and the person with whom you are in conflict. If you don't have a picture of the person(s) involved write your name and theirs on a piece of paper.

Directions:

1. Cleanse your sacred space.

2. Place both candles side by side on top of the mirror.

3. Light the candles focusing your mind on the words *peace* and *harmony*.

4. Draw a heart around the picture of you and the person.

5. Write the words "peace" and "harmony" on the back of the picture or paper.

6. Speak the following mantra out loud three times

> *This conflict is clouding my heart and my mind*
>
> *Cause no more distress, let's all be kind.*
>
> *Themis, Pasithea, shall sanctify*
>
> *Love and peace Mother Moon will amplify.*

So mote it be.

7. Set the picture and paper aflame and let them burn all the way on top of the mirror.

8. Take a few drops of moon-blessed water and mix it into the ashes.

9. Form a heart with the wet ashes.

10. Thank the Moon Goddess.

11. Let the heart dry overnight.

12. Dig a small hole in the dirt and bury the ashes, along with any conflict and resentments you may feel.

13. Take the mirror off the lunar altar. It did its job by multiplying the power of the candles and reflecting the Moon's vibrational energies into your spell.

ENERGY CLEANSING RITUAL

What You'll Need:

- Waxing crescent moon
- Cinnamon stick
- Clear quartz crystal
- White candle
- Paper and pen

Direction:

1. Write a list of any negative forces in your life that you are ready to release on a piece of paper.
2. Fold the paper up and put it on your lunar altar in front of you.

3. Light your candle.
4. Hold your cinnamon stick in the flame until it starts smoking.
5. Trace the lines of your body with the cinnamon stick smoke, over and around your head, down to your shoulders, around your arms and torso, down and around your legs, back, and over your feet. You may have to keep relighting your cinnamon stick, if you have no luck at all getting the cinnamon stick to smoke, place it on your altar and complete those steps with a sage or palo alto bundle.
6. While gazing in the flame of your candle, slow your thinking and relax your mind. Spend a full 60 seconds taking the deepest breaths you can in through your nose and into your belly before releasing it out through your mouth.
7. Visualize all and any negativity forming into a black cloud of smoke billowing up from your deepest core as you are slowly breathing in and being forced from your body and your surroundings—with the force of your exhale—out into the atmosphere, past the earth, and disintegrated by the Moon.
8. Repeat steps 6 and 7 until it feels tangible and real.
9. Be done with the list on your paper by burning it thoroughly.
10. Thank the goddesses and gods of the Moon for a thorough deep cleansing.
11. Notice how light you feel on your feet and smile.

FRANK BAWDOE

ENEMY PROTECTION SPELL

What You'll Need:

- Waxing crescent moon
- A black candle
- A white candle
- Lavender and rose essential oils
- 4 small glass jars
- Dried lemon peel, basil, black salt, and rice.

Directions:

1. On the morning of the true waxing crescent moon, smudge your house in its entirety.

2. Fill each of the four jars with the dried lemon peels, basil, and black salt. You can make the black salt by mixing the ashes from your sage bundle with the white sea salt.

3. Place them on your lunar altar or on a windowsill where they can absorb the Moon's energy.

4. Place them in a diamond pattern to represent the four cardinal directions. The lavender will bring you peace and the basil and black salt will ward off and protect you from your enemies. The rice brings you good luck and the lemon boosts the powers of each ingredient.

5. Let them charge under the waxing crescent moon overnight.

6. The next day, in the morning, place one candle in between the jars on your altar.

7. Anoint your candles with the lavender and rose oils.

8. Light the black candle to banish evil and protect you from any enemies.

9. Light the white candle to purify your thoughts and your environment.

10. With your intentions set in clarity, cast your spell:

> *Protect this house from from danger and dirt*
>
> *Get rid of my enemies plans to hurt*
>
> *Fill me with strength and the power to see*
>
> *And anything harmful aimed at me*
>
> *So mote it be*

11. Let both candles burn down completely and then bury the wax under the Moon in your yard.

12. Keep the jars on your altar until the next lunar phase.

13. Pour the contents of the jars into an abalone shell and spread them around the outskirts of your home to ward off your enemies.

5

FIRST QUARTER MOON SPELLS FOR MAKING DECISIONS

The first quarter moon looks like a half pie, and it is a time to face the obstacles and challenges in your path, to focus on the elements that matter in this phase and on reaching your goals. Other spells that work during this phase include creative magic, such as divination, growth, motivation, and strength. During the first quarter moon phase, visualization is a great way to get creative with your lunar magic. Start out with simple lunar meditations, visualizing your intentions for this particular lunar phase.

Also, for this particular lunar phase, practice your breathing with the full intention of relaxing. Breathe deep into your belly and slowly exhale. Deep breathing can reset the mind and body. Studies have revealed that deep breathing restores balance to the central nervous system and the body's stress response, calms agitation, and lowers anxiety levels (Brown & Gerberg, 2012). Breathe in and count to four, and then hold your breath and count to four, and exhale counting to four 4-4-4, it's easy.

First Quarter Ritual Idea

SACRED WATER RITUAL

What You'll Need:

- First quarter moon
- Glass of spring water
- Natural salt
- A burned piece of incense

Directions:

1. Put the salt and the incense into the glass of water.
2. Place the glass in the center of your lunar altar and start the ritual.
3. Mediate and review your special intentions.

HEALTHY HABITS SPELL

The first quarter moon is in transition between a new and full moon. It is a time for refinement and adjustment. Health wise, nutritional challenges may occur and you may find yourself struggling to eat healthy. Keep a positive mindset and treat yourself kindly. It is a good time for readjusting your health goals and maybe upping the ante and challenging yourself a bit more. Maybe cut down on your alcohol or caffeine intake, or shop for organic foods.

Note: The color corresponding with a first quarter moon is yellow, and its incense is poplar.

What You'll Need:

- First quarter moon
- Light blue cloth
- An apple
- A light blue candle
- Poplar incense
- Rose essential oil

Directions:

1. On the evening of the first quarter moon

2. Cleanse your lunar altar

3. Anoint your light blue candle with the rose essential oil

4. Light your incense

5. Slice your apple in half to represent the moon.

6. Chant the following aloud.

> *Mother Moon, I'm here to say*
>
> *I believe in an apple a day.*
>
> *Half for me and half for you*
>
> *I'll wrap your half in a very light blue.*
>
> *Bring to me healthy habits to stay*
>
> *I feel them filling me with your light blue rays.*
>
> *So mote it be.*

7. Eat your half of the apple

8. Wrap the other half of the apple in the blue cloth

9. Bury the blue cloth containing the half apple in the ground under the moon.

10. Thank Mother Moon and snuff out your candle to close the spell.

MENTAL CLARITY SPELL

This spell is best cast during a first quarter moon and using items that correspond with the element air.

What You'll Need:

- First quarter moon
- Yellow candle
- Feathers
- Lemons
- Cardamon
- Lemongrass incense

- Pen and paper
- A bowl of clear spring water
- Scissors

Directions:

1. Cleanse your lunar altar

2. Adorn your altar with feathers, lemons, cardamom, and any items that resonate with you and correspond with the element air.

3. Carve or scribe this sigil for mental clarity in your yellow candle:

4. Put your bowl of water in front of your candle in the center of your lunar altar.

5. Light your yellow candle and speak out loud

> *I call upon the Moon Goddess to ask for your help.*
>
> *Remove my distractions, give clarity to myself.*
>
> *Oh thank you, oh Moon, for healing my mind.*
>
> *All mental distractions are now left behind.*
>
> *As it is and should be.*

6. Relax your mind and meditate on your bowl of water

7. As thoughts come into your mind, jot them down and then release them from your mind.

8. After each thought has come and gone, refocus on your water bowl and your candle. If any intrusive thoughts enter your mind, fan them away with a feather.

9. Meditate and continue the ritual for thirty minutes, a *full* thirty minutes or longer, until your mind is clear.

10. Look at your list and then cut the page so that each item is on its own strip of paper.

11. Starting with the least important item, burn them one by one, visualizing the smoke on its way to the moon.

12. Thank the Moon Goddess and either snuff or let your candle burn all the way down to close the spell.

MAKE THE RIGHT DECISION SPELL

Your subconscious mind is governed by the moon; that part of yourself that is felt at the deepest soulful level and is often the part most difficult to express. Using the lunar energetic shift as a roadmap for planning your goals will help you manifest decisions for living your best life. Afterall, the word lunatic, which now means crazy, first meant deep lovers of the moon. With the first quarter moon, you are able to move toward implementing your new moon intentions. In other words, now is the time for decision making. Use this phase of the Moon's momentum to overcome any obstacles you may be facing along the way. You can change and add things that need to be readjusted with the intentions you have for the new moon during the first quarter moon phase. The gods and goddesses of the

Universe are allowing you to edit your intentions according to your needs and lifestyle.

What You'll Need:

- First quarter moon
- Pen and paper
- An old key

Directions:

1. Cleanse your lunar altar.

2. Draw the capital letter Y on a piece of paper to symbolize a fork in the road.

3. You are calling upon the powers of the Maiden aspect of the Moon. At night during the first quarter moon—just before you go to bed—place the old key that you don't need anymore over the letter Y on your altar and speak three times:

> *I have decisions to make*
>
> *Tell me which path to take.*
>
> *With this key my mind straightens*
>
> *To seek the wisdom of the Maiden.*
>
> *So mote it be.*

4. Go straight to bed. You will either awaken with your answer or you will dream prophetically.

FRANK BAWDOE

PIVOT SPELL

Everything doesn't always go the way we want it to, or the way we think it is going to go. Sometimes life takes a sudden turn in the wrong direction, and you can either change course entirely or take a step back and get back on track. Whichever path you decide to take, the best thing you can do is enjoy the scenery. This spell will help you to pivot and enjoy the scenery, either way you turn.

What You'll Need:

- First quarter moon
- Light blue candle
- Tongs
- Small piece of blue paper
- Blue ink pen
- White paper
- Black paper
- Fireproof container or cauldron
- Blue attire
- Frankincense

Directions:

1. One one side of the small piece of blue paper, write down the path or direction you have been heading.

2. On the other side of the small blue piece of paper, write down an obstacle or struggle that has revealed itself to you, requiring you to make a pivotal decision.

3. Place the blue paper with your writings in between the white and black paper.

4. Form a makeshift folder out of the papers by bending the edges together, holding the blue paper in between them.

5. Light the papers on fire over your blue candle, using tongs for safety.

6. Speak the following out loud.

> *First quarter moon, show me the way.*
>
> *So I may pivot accordingly today.*
>
> *So mote it be.*

7. After the ashes have cooled, take them outside and toss them toward the Moon.

8. Let your candle burn or snuff it out, thank Mother Moon and close the spell.

TO TELL THE TRUTH

What You'll Need:

- First quarter moon
- White candle
- Cauldron or fireproof container
- Lighter or matches
- A strand of the person's hair you want to speak the truth
- Pen and paper

Directions:

1. Place your white candle in the center of your lunar altar

2. Write the name or names of the people from whom you are seeking the truth

3. Place the strand of hair in the piece of paper with their name(s) on it and fold it closed before placing it in the cauldron and speak the following out loud.

> *First quarter moon, help me now.*
>
> *I seek the truth yet to be found.*
>
> *For under your magic today there lies*
>
> *The truth to be told to open my eyes.*
>
> *Your magic is strong and like no other*
>
> *To have this person show their true colors.*
>
> *So mote it be.*

4. Burn the paper in your cauldron while focusing on the flame and your intention.

5. Let the paper burn all the way to ash.

6. Thank Mother Moon and close the spell.

6

WAXING GIBBOUS MOON SPELLS FOR GETTING SPECIFIC

A waxing gibbous moons feels more energetic; it is a time to tie up loose ends, develop, and achieve your desired results. Spellwise, it's a time for constructive magic.

FRANK BAWDOE

WAXING GIBBOUS RITUAL

What You'll Need:

- Waxing gibbous moon
- A yellow candle
- A star anise
- 2 pinches of dried rosemary
- Mortar and pestle

Directions:

1. Blend your frankincense, star anise, and dried rosemary with your mortar and pestle.
2. Place the blend in a small jar or herb container in the middle of your lunar altar.
3. Light your yellow candle.
4. Focus your intention into the flame and speak the following out loud.

Oh Maiden Moon, hear my plea.

Listen please unto me.

As you grow, my spells enhance.

Under your light, my magic will dance.

Speak to me with clear and loud signs.

Let me share in your great Maiden mind.

So mote it be.

PERSONIFICATION SPELL

When we see the waxing gibbous moon rising in the night, it is the goddess Selene waving hello from her chariot of silver drawn by two white horses. Selene is the personification of the moon itself, and her powers correspond with intuition, dreams, emotions, healing, and much more.

What You'll Need:

- A picture of the waxing gibbous moon
- Two moonstone crystals, symbolizing Selene
- Any type of horse figurines, especially in white or silver if possible.
- Moon-blessed water
- A silver bowl
- A handwritten by you poem dedicated to Selene
- Cleansed bathtub
- Rose petals
- A silver or white robe

Directions:

1. Cleanse your lunar altar with sage and dedicate your sacred altar to Selene. Tell her you built it in her honor.

2. Place your moonstones and blessed water on the altar.

3. Read your poem out loud to her.

4. Fill your silver bowl with the moon-blessed water

5. Prepare a bath and float your rose petals

6. Pour your moon-blessed water from the silver bowl into the tub

7. Speak the following out loud.

> *Goddess of the Moon, Selene, may your love and moonlight fill my needs.*
>
> *I see you personified*
>
> *In love and the water's tides.*
>
> *Connect me to you, for you are so wise.*
>
> *So mote it be.*

8. Take a ritual bath in honor of Selene, the goddess of the Moon.

9. Wear a silver robe in her honor for the rest of the night.

COMMUNICATION SPELL

Crystals harness the power of the waxing gibbous moon; specifically, lapis lazuli is known as the "stone of truth." It helps you to communicate clearly, honestly, and effectively both with yourself and with others. Its name comes from the Persian and Latin word meaning "blue stone." Blue is also the color of the throat chakra, which corresponds with your abilities for expressing yourself. It is also a protective gem against the negative thoughts and words of others. Adding clear quartz and amethyst to your lunar altar while charging your lapis lazuli with moon-blessed water will boot the spell's energy. It is always good to keep a few gallons of moon-blessed water around, and you can even freeze it to make ice cubes.

What You'll Need:

- Waxing gibbous moon
- A piece lapis lazuli
- A amethyst

- 1 or more clear quartz crystals
- A yellow or white candle

Directions:

1. Cleanse your lunar altar.

2. Place the clear quartz crystal and the amethyst crystal in front of your yellow or white candle and light the candle.

3. Hold the lapis lazuli cupped in both hands.

4. Close your eyes and deep breathe.

5. Visualize the moonbeams shooting down from the sky and into the lapis lazuli.

6. Picture yourself feeling satisfied and relieved about how easy it is for you to have a conversation.

7. See the positive energy flowing from the Moon into the crystal and through your hands while saying the following out loud three times.

> *I communicate effectively and clearly from the essence of truth.*
>
> *My conversations will no longer seem aloof.*
>
> *So mote it be.*

8. When you feel the energy has fully charged the crystal, place it near the clear quartz and amethyst crystals and leave all three there with the candle burning for at least two hours.

9. Keep the lapis lazuli stone with you, where it will be ready to help you with your conversations.

POSITIVITY SPELL JAR

Jasmine flowers are known to absorb and infuse many energies—lunar magic, friendship, spiritual connections, and so much more.

What You'll Need:

- Waxing gibbous moon
- Jar that has been charged in moonlight to remove any negative energies.
- A white candle for balance and harmony.
- 4 grams of jasmine flowers
- 4 grams chamomile flowers
- 4 grams pink himalayan salt
- 4 grams sunflower petals for protection and energy
- 4 grams of rose petals for domestic happiness
- 4 grams of sea salt for cleansing and protection
- 4 grams coffee grounds for positive energy and peace
- 4 grams cinnamon for protection
- 4 grams ginger for prosperity and positivity
- 4 grams cloves for protection
- 4 grams vanilla beans for positivity and energy

Directions:

1. Focus on the attributes of each item as you put them in your jar. The attributes are listed next to the ingredients above.

2. Layer them according to your intuition.

3. Seal the jar with wax or tightly with the lip.

4. Place your hands over the lid.

5. Say the following out loud three times.

   Mother Moon, bless this jar with happiness, protection, energy, and positivity.

   So mote it be.

6. Meditate under the waxing gibbous moon, letting its energy flow into the jar.

7. Feel your energy, charged from the moon, flowing through your hands into the lid and into the jar.

8. Snuff out your candle and close the spell.

9. Keep the jar on your lunar altar until the next lunar phase, then keep it somewhere that you can see it often, filling you with positivity the way you filled it.

INSPIRATIONAL MOON SPELL

Spells for inspiration can help your creativity and motivation start flowing with the life of the moonlit stars. This spell will provide you with the inspiration for starting something you have been dreaming of—or inspire new motivation for a project or situation you are already in the middle of doing.

Sometimes you need a little additional energy to get inspiration going, and this simple spell uses some fire to make that happen.

What You'll Need:

- Waxing gibbous moon
- Yellow candle
- Flame proof container or surface

- Two dry sprigs of mint

Directions:

1. Light your yellow candle and speak the following out loud.

Fuse and spark ignite my heart

In its fuse, find my muse

Within its flame, inspiration untamed

Smoke in the air, time to care and take a dare

So mote it be.

2. Hole a mint sprig in your right hand and light it in the flame of your yellow candle.

3. Hold them out in front of your lunar altar.

4. As they smolder and the smoke rises toward Mother Moon, repeat the chant two more times.

5. Let the ashes fall into your abalone shell.

6. Take the ashes outside and toss them toward the Moon, visualizing her dancing around and collecting each piece while she returns your worship with inspiration.

7. Snuff your candle and express your gratitude to the moon goddess of inspiration and close the spell.

RECLAIM PERSONAL POWER SPELL

This spell is a recovery ritual for reclaiming your personal power. It provides you with the ability to identify all of the times where situations and people zapped your powers and energy and allows you to reclaim them. There is not ill intent or anger involved in this ritual, it simply helps you to look at the past few months to a year and reclaim the personal power that is rightfully yours

The waxing gibbous moon will guide you to a place of neutrality, so you can come to understand that providing people your anger is giving them power over you. It affords you a place of neutrality, so if need be, repeat the spell as often as necessary as a training exercise.

What You'll Need:

- Waxing gibbous moon
- Two bowls
- Two red candles as red corresponds with power
- A collection of small items such as pebbles, small crystals, beads, leaves
- Moon incense
- Pen and paper

Directions:

1. Set up your lunar altar with one candle to the left and one to the right.
2. Place your two bowls in a straight line, one close to you and one further away.
3. Fill the bowl furthest from you with your small items—not the pen and paper.
4. The items in the bowl furthest from you represent your energetic powers that you will be working toward returning them to you, so make sure you have plenty of these small items.
5. Light your moon incense and your candles.
6. Find your stillness through breathing and relaxing.

7. You are creating a sacred space for safety, comfort, and renewal.
8. Meditate on retrieving your personal powers. Feel the magic of the waxing gibbous moon's healing energy
9. Write down the circumstances causing you the need to reclaim your powers. Write down specifically where you think they are hiding.
10. Reach into the bowl with your items—the one furthest away—and pick one item.
11. Hold it in your hand and name the person, situation, or moment that you are reclaiming your energy and power from. For instance, "I am taking my power back from_____"
12. Place the item in the closest bowl to you and concentrate on feeling its energy, fueled by the moon, rushing back and filling you with power.
13. Continue until you have reclaimed all of your power and transferred each item.
14. You can take a break and go back to transferring items if you start to feel fatigued. This spell needs to be cast after a good night's sleep, or after you have taken a nap on the day of the waxing gibbous moon.

PROSPERITY SPELL

Using the waxing gibbous moon for prosperity is like turning on a powerful magnet for good luck. Do the work on your part and Mother Moon will respond with prosperity like you have never seen before.

What You'll Need:

- Waxing gibbous moon
- Anthem or a penknife
- A green candle
- Green aventurine, the prosperity stone
- Green citrine for positivity

Directions:

1. Carve or scribe the exact type of prosperity or amount of money you wish to manifest on the side of your green candle. Make it something within your reach.
2. Place the candle in the middle of your lunar altar and light it.
3. Place the green citrine and the green aventurine on each side of your candle
4. Light your candle and spend a few moments with the image in your mind of how your life will change with great prosperity as if it has already happened.
5. Blow the candle out.
6. Relight the candle and conduct the ritual every night at the same time while the moon is waxing.
7. By the end of the week, you will see things starting to change for the better.

STRENGTHEN MY LOVE SPELL

Faithfulness and trust are complex and inborn needs. Love relationships require mutual respect and compromise. Usually, when there is a weakness in a relationship, it is due to one or both of the individual's insecurities. For this spell, you will be using crystals to harness the waxing gibbous moon's energy to strengthen you and your loved one's bond.

What You'll Need:

- Waxing gibbous moon
- Poppy seeds
- Rosemary
- Cardamom
- Sodalite
- Lapis lazuli
- A dark blue or black drawstring pouch

Directions:

1. Scatter one-half of the poppy seeds over your lover's footprints.

2. Put the rest of the poppy seeds in the pouch.

3. Add some cardamom to a meal you are enjoying together at the same time.

4. Hold a lapis lazuli crystal in one hand and the sodalite crystal in the other hand.

5. Close your eyes and chant the following out loud.

> *I trust our love; our bond is true.*
>
> *Under this moon, our love strengthens too.*
>
> *Our love is one that time cannot cheat.*
>
> *It's strong and powerful, no challenge can beat.*
>
> *So mote it be.*

6. Put all of the ingredients in the pouch and place it on your lunar altar until the next lunar cycle. Repeat the spell each waxing gibbous moon phase until you feel the spell is complete.

7

FULL MOON SPELLS FOR CELEBRATION, GLOW, AND REFLECTION

Full moons attract all good things to you and heal you from the past emotional pains. It can be constructive and destructive, banishing unwanted energies and influences from your life, performing divination magic, creating protection spells.

Full Moon Ritual Idea for divination and reading. It is a time to communicate with spirits and deities. Sit down with a view of the full moon and start a ritual meditation. Concentrate on your intentions and on receiving guidance from the goddess, and after you're done, you need to ground yourself. Eating something heavy helps with this.

SMOKE CLEANSING RITUAL

What You'll Need:

- Full moon
- Sage
- Palo santo

Directions:

- Ceremoniously cleanse away any negative energies hanging around you, your home, and your electronic devices.

Note: Palo santo and white sage are at risk of over-harvesting due to their popularity and face the potential for extinction. Try growing your own sage to make bundles and source responsibly.

DREAM VISION SPELL

What You'll Need:

- Full moon
- Blue ink pen
- Small piece of white paper
- Clear quartz crystal

- White round candle

Directions:

1. Cleanse your lunar altar

2. Decorate your altar with any items and written symbols that honor the full moon.

3. Carve a question mark into the candle.

4. Place your candle in the middle of your altar.

5. Place your four clear quartz crystals symbolizing the cardinal directions.

6. Light your white candle.

7. Write down a question you desire the answer for, and it can be regarding anything occupying your thoughts.

8. Fold it in half and speak the following out loud.

> *Mother Moon Goddess, as I travel the astral realm,*
>
> *I wish to know [speak your question].*
>
> *My will be done.*
>
> *So mote it be.*

9. Leave the piece of paper folded under the candle overnight, make sure the candle is in a safe place to burn and let it burn while you sleep, and you will awaken with your answer.

RITUAL STEPS FOR HARVESTING FULL MOON BLISS

1. Turn off all devices.

2. Breathe six long breaths in silence under the full moon, where you have a clear view of it.

3. Focus on the full moon's cleansing effects.

4. Light a white candle and a blue candle. This is best if you can make an outdoor lunar altar. This will enhance your intuition and help you to release all negativity.

5. Write with a blue pen on white paper any of your troubles. For instance, problems with addiction, bad situations, or even a negative person in your life. Writing things down makes your intentions for harvesting a blissful life much more clear.

6. Visualize your blissfulness. Picture your life being blissful. Let your soul swell with blissfulness the full moon offers you.

7. Ask the Mother Moon for forgiveness out loud. This mantra is for forgiving someone else or yourself.

   I forgive myself or [person's/institution/ etc.]

So mote it be.

8. Feel all of the negativity leave your body as your chakras align with the full moon.

9. Express your gratitude and close the spell.

LUNAR REJUVENATION SPELL

What You'll Need:

- Full moon
- Rose quartz crystal
- Light purple altar cloth
- Celestial music, there are many ethereal soundtracks available free online
- Anthame
- Moon incense or jasmine incense
- A glass of wine or punch
- Shot glass or small cup
- Velvet drawstring pouch in dark blue or black

Directions:

1. Take a ritual cleansing bath.
2. Cleanse your lunar altar.
3. Cast your circle around your altar.
4. Light your moon or jasmine incense and charge your crystal with the smoke. Ask your crystal to harness the energy of the full moon and bring it to you.
5. Sit on the ground and enter into a meditative state, checking your body for all emotional awareness. It feels like a tugging sense or a heaviness.
6. Symbolize severing your mind and body from that heaviness with your anthem. Remember this is symbolic, be very careful to hold your anthem far from your body.
7. Visualize the full moon's light pulsating over you.
8. Visualize the full moon's glow entering into your body, telling you, "you are alive!"

9. Pick up your crystal and visualize the Moon's remaining energy drawn into it.
10. Place the crystal in the bag and carry it with you, looking at it every evening under the full moon throughout this lunar phase.
11. Toast your glass of wine or punch to the Mother Moon and tell her out loud how rejuvenated you feel.
12. Pour a small amount of wine into a cup or shot glass and place it on your altar.
13. Open the circle and the spell is completed.

SELF-LOVE CELEBRATION SPELL

What You'll Need:

- Pen or marker
- A leaf from outside
- Purple candle
- Lighter
- Rose quartz crystals
- Pink altar cloth
- Sage
- Fireproof glass or mirror

Directions:

1. Turn off and unplug anything not involved in your full moon magic.

2. Create a sacred space with your lunar altar in the middle outside under the full moon.

3. Smudge all of your items, yourself, and your sacred space.

4. Light your purple candle

5. Make sure you are under the full moon and that it is shining down on your space. If it's raining, open all of your curtains and set your altar close to the window.

6. On your fallen leaf, write down what you want to release and what you want to attract.

7. On a piece of paper write three affirmations:

> *"I am strong."*
>
> *"I am beautiful."*
>
> *"I am wise."*
>
> *"I am happy with who I am."*
>
> *"I love me."*

8. Speak each affirmation out loud.

9. Burn the paper and visualize the full moon inhaling the smoke and returning to you in the form of a hugging sensation encircling your entire body.

10. Burn the leaf.

11. Take the ashes from the leaf and throw them in the air, visualizing Mother Moon and Mother Nature together, telling you to love and care for yourself the way they do.

8

WANING GIBBOUS MOON SPELLS FOR EXPRESSING GRATITUDE

A waning gibbous moon means a decrease in anything negative or unneeded. Its magic is good for banishing spells, cleaning up your living space, cleaning magic, removing curses, cleansing spells, undoing bindings, and removing negativity.

Waning Gibbous Ritual Idea

Write down a list of all your fears, troubles, insecurities. For this ritual, you can burn the paper while surrendering to the moon's power as you banish and relinquish those doubts, and move toward getting what you need and deserve.

EMBRACING OBSTACLES SPELL

What You'll Need:

- Waning gibbous moon
- A small, hand-held mirror
- An acorn or some other type of berry or nut that has fallen from a tree
- A piece of yarn tied in a loose knot
- A black candle

Directions:

1. Cleanse your lunar altar.

2. Place your mirror in the middle of your altar.

3. Place your knotted yarn and berry in the middle of your mirror.

4. Light your candle.

5. Speak the following out loud.

> *Mirror, Mirror, on my Altar,*
>
> *Bless me Moon so I won't falter.*
>
> *Obstacles come and then they go.*
>
> *My inner strength is all I know.*
>
> *So mote it be.*

6. Pick up your yarn, untie the knot, and place it back on your altar.

7. Take the acorn or berry and bury it in the back yard or somewhere close to your dwelling.

8. Look at yourself in the mirror and repeat the chant.

9. Snuff out your candle and close the spell.

HONOR THY ANGER SPELL

What You'll Need:

- A black candle
- A red candle
- A white candle
- A light blue candle
- A small, white tea candle

Directions:

1. Place all four candles on your lunar altar with the small white tea candle in the middle.

2. Light your candles and say the following out loud five times.

Anger is reality.

Anger is protection.

Anger is human.

Anger is a message from the Universe.

Anger is energy.

Anger is power.

3. Blow out the tea candle and let the other four burn for one hour.

4. After the hour is up, snuff the candles out and close the spell.

HONORING A RELATIONSHIP SPELL

What You'll Need:

- Waning gibbous moon
- Two bundles of parsley
- A white thread
- A red Candle
- 2 lighters

Directions:

1. Sit together with your partner under a waning gibbous moon.
2. Each of you strike your lighters and light the candle together.

3. Each of you wrap the string around the base of the parsley nine times
4. Both of you pick up the bundle of parsley you each wrapped.
5. Stand facing each other.
6. While you are passing your parsley bundles to each other, tell each other three things you are grateful for in the relationship.
7. Lay the parsley bundle you received next to you on the altar
8. Let the candle burn all the way in a safe place, or snuff it out while holding hands and complete the spell.

THANKSGIVING RITUAL DURING WANING GIBBOUS MOON

What You'll Need:

- Waning Gibbous Moon
- Chair
- Orange candle
- Jasmine incense
- Pen and paper

Directions:

1. Create Sacred Space and light the orange candle and the jasmine incense.
2. Write down what you are grateful for, including qualities you like in yourself, your achievements, your obstacles, for being free, for Mother Moon, and for your family.
3. List your intentions for the next lunar phase.

4. Sit on the chair and connect with the Moon in meditation. Visualize yourself like you are a flower, opening up to the Moon, and the Moon is watering you with its silver light.
5. Read out loud through your gratitude list and think about the feelings associated with each item. The words are the framework holding together the energy you are manifesting for the ritual. Focus intently on conjuring up emotions of gratitude. This opens up channels for the Moon's magic to infiltrate your spirit.
6. Sit for thirty minutes with this feeling, let it overflow you with happiness and joy.
7. Set an intention for the good of someone else.
8. Thank the Moon, Mother Earth, the Elements, and any other celestial beings you can think of.
9. Snuff the candle and close the ritual.

MINIMALISM MOON SPELL

Directions:

1. Pick eleven days and take notice of the number eleven everywhere you go.
2. Keep a journal of everything you have seen with the number eleven involved.
3. When you see 11 11 or 1111 you will know your intuition is elevated.

THANKING MOTHER EARTH SPELL

What You'll Need:

- Waning gibbous moon
- Garden soil
- Bowl
- Dried leaves
- Coffee grounds
- A green or brown candle
- A blue candle
- A yellow candle
- Spring water in a spouted container

Directions:

1. Place your garden soil in the bowl on your outdoor lunar altar

2. Add in your coffee grounds and mix together well.

3. Draw a river or jungle path with your finger through the dirt

4. Inscribe your blue candle with the Laguz rune symbol for water and Ansuz rune symbol for air.

5. Inscribe your brown candle with the Inguz the rune symbol for earth.

6. Inscribe your yellow candle with Kenaz, the rune symbol for fire.

7. Add your spring water.

8. Say out loud:

> *Mother Earth holds the water.*
>
> *It's healing blue.*
>
> *She holds the sand*
>
> *and heals the land*

with all that's green.

Please bless her, Mother Moon

with all that is clean.

So mote it be.

9. Stir the water into the dirt

10. Continue chanting until the soil is mixed and damp.

11. Sprinkle some of the soil onto the Earth to carry your spell's intention.

12. Keep the soil mixture on your altar in a sealed container.

13. Whenever you see something unkind to nature, sprinkle some of the dirt either where it happened or symbolically in your own yard.

9

WANING CRESCENT MOON FOR SURRENDER AND RELEASE

A waning crescent moon is a time of restoration, healing, meditating, and nurturing yourself. Use it to recuperate, rest, and recharge your energy. This phase will help you find balance and slow down to reflect on the past and help you to resolve any struggles so you may move forward.

DARK GODDESS RITUAL

What You'll Need:

- Three black candles
- Lighter
- Ash or soot, you can use your incense or sage ash for extra *umph*
- Hand mirror
- Black obsidian crystal
- Homemade cookies or fresh flowers, I like making the cookies
- Offerings for the goddess
- Witch's wand

Directions:

1. Cleanse your lunar altar with sage and keep the ash.

2. Place your black obsidian crystal on the mirror

3. Surround the mirror and the crystal with the candles

4. Light your three black candles and notice the reflection of the black candles as representing the dark goddess.

5. Speak the following out loud.

> *I invoke you, Dark Goddess of the Moon, into my sacred space to grant me the power of compassion and to instill upon me a deep knowledge of divine magic. I ask that you illuminate my journey. So mote it be.*

6. Collect the ash in your abalone shell.

7. Hold the shell up to the sky and say the chant again.

8. Toss the ash in the air and visualize the dark goddess reaching with very long arms dressed in black silk to gather the ash and return a silver streak of light enveloping your mind, your body, and your soul.

9. Snuff your candles and close the spell.

BANISH MY ALCOHOL ADDICTION SPELL

What You'll Need:

- Waning crescent moon
- A black candle
- A white candle
- Totem (fingernails, toenails, lock of hair, or

something they have worn on their body) of the person if it is not you.
- Pen and paper

Directions:

1. Place the white candle in the center of your lunar altar.

2. Place the black candle on the west side of the white candle

3. Place the totem next to the white candle on the east side.

4. Write down the exact outcome you desire as if it has already occurred.

> *I did not drink today.*
>
> *I did not drink one day at a time.*
>
> *I am healthy.*
>
> *I am nourished.*
>
> *Mother Moon, banish my desire for alcohol.*
>
> *So mote it be.*

5. Tear the paper up in thirteen pieces.

6. Place the crumbled pieces of paper in a row heading west from the black candle.

7. Light both candles, visualizing what a clean and sober life would be. Feel the freedom from your vice picture the happiness in your loved ones.

8. Burn the first crumbled paper nearest to the black candle.

9. Move the black candle over the space where the burned paper sat away from the white candle.

10. For thirteen nights, burn one piece and move the cande. Continue until all of the crumbled pieces are burned and the black candle is far away from the white candle.

11. Notice you have thirteen days sober.

12. Repeat the entire ritual for as long as you need.

YOU NEED TO CUT THE CORD SPELL

What You'll Need:

- Waning crescent moon
- 3 Pieces of yarn—red, white, and blue
- Red: the connection and passion that binds you
- White: your willingness and intention to bring the situation to light.
- Blue: welcoming the knowledge during and after the ritual.
- A white candle
- A bowl of water
- A white sage bundle
- Scissors

Directions:

1. Sit outside under the moon where you will have zero interruptions.

2. Place the white candle on your outdoor lunar altar in front of you. If you can find a tree stump or a flat rock, it would enhance your mood and therefore your magic.

3. Meditate on the white candle, symbolizing divine pure light. It mirrors the flame and harnesses the energy of the waning crescent moon.

4. Visualize your intentions passing through the flame, guided by the Moon's vibrational energy.

5. Light your sage bundle and smudge yourself, your altar, and the area around you.

6. Make three, 9-inch sections of yarn in red, white, and blue with the scissors, symbolizing cutting the cord.

7. Braid the three strands of yarn and tie a small knot at the ends.

8. Clear your mind, harness the Moon's infinite power, and pour all of your raw energy and intention into the braided cord.

9. Say out loud

> *It is my intention to cut the cord.*
>
> *It's this relationship I cannot afford.*
>
> *It's time for me to cut all ties.*
>
> *It's time for me to say goodbye.*
>
> *I feel this with all of my might.*
>
> *Please fill the space with your gorgeous moonlight.*
>
> *So mote it be.*

10. While you are holding the strands, put all of your questions, feelings, and frustrations into the cord.

11. Let any anger and sadness you feel rise inside of you meet your intention, including the shedding of tears, knowing they are released and cannot hijack your being any longer.

12. Sit holding the cord until you have released all pent up emotions and are left with a sense of utter relaxation.

13. Say the following out loud.

> *I have let you go.*
>
> *This you should know.*
>
> *The cord is cut.*
>
> *This pathway is shut.*
>
> *For me, for you, I forgive.*
>
> *With peace in my heart, I can now live.*
>
> *So mote it be.*

14. Allow the cord to burn in the candle flame.

15. Dip your hands in the now moon-blessed water and shake them dry, symbolizing good riddance.

16. Smudge yourself again after the ritual

17. Put out the candle and go in peace.

FINAL THOUGHTS

It is no surprise the Wiccans, witches, and pagans love the Moon—and so does most of humanity. Hopefully, you have learned a great deal about how to harness the powers of the lunar phases and in the process how to elevate all of your spells with her magic. Throughout this book, the one constant other than the Moon itself, is the importance of

FINAL THOUGHTS

your lunar altar. It is specifically dedicated to each phase of the Moon with corresponding items, colors, herbs, candles, crystals, and essential oils.

One of the many topics covered in *Moon Spells: Your Complete Guide to the Hidden Power of Lunar Phases, Wiccan Magic, Rituals, and Witchcraft* is that our internal biological rhythms are connected to Moon's cycle. Gaining an intimate relationship with the Moon and her energies is essential to any witchcraft practice. If she can control the tides of the great waters on Earth, she surely holds great and powerful magic. Magic that you can harness just by asking her, acknowledging her, and of course honoring her.

I hope that you enjoy this book as much as I enjoyed writing it. If you did, it would be wonderful if you could take a short minute and leave a review on Amazon, as your kind feedback is much appreciated and so very important.

Thank you.

REFERENCES

Andrews, R. (2018). The moon is electric, especially when it's full. *National Geographic Magazine.* https://www.nationalgeographic.com/science/article/news-full-moon-electric-ionosphere-nasa-artemis-space

Brown, R. & Gerbarg, P. (2012). The healing power of the breath: Simple techniques to reduce stress and anxiety, enhance concentration, and balance your emotions. *Shambhala, Boston.* ISBN: 10-1590309022

Cajochen. C., Altanay-Ekici, S., M., Münch, Frey, S., Knoblauch, V., & Wirz-Justice, A. (2013). Evidence that the lunar cycle influences human sleep. *Current Biology (23)*15, P1485-1488. https://www.cell.com/current-biology/fulltext/S0960-9822(13)00754-9

Criger, C. (2021). Pentacle (Wiccan). *Grove Oklahoma.com.* https://www.cityofgroveok.gov/building/page/pentacle-wiccan

Daley, J. (2019). Oysters 0pen and close their shells as the moon wanes and waxes. *Smithsonian Magazine.*

REFERENCES

https://www.smithsonianmag.com/smart-news/oysters-sync-lunar-cycle-180971230/

Dragonsong, E. (2021). The power of the Moon. *Wicca Spirituality.* https://www.wicca-spirituality.com/power-moon.html

Dual Crossroads. (2021). *The history and symbolism of the pentagram.* https://www.dualcrossroads.com/post/the-history-and-symbolism-of-the-pentagram

Fellizar, K. & Kahn, N. (2021). Astrologers explain how the moon can affect your mood. *Bustle Magazine.* https://www.bustle.com/life/6-weird-ways-the-moon-can-affect-your-mood-17020547

Gannon, M. (2013). A bewitching history: Why witches ride broomsticks. *LiveScience.com.* https://www.livescience.com/40828-why-witches-ride-broomsticks.html

Gardner, G. (1950). The Gardnerian Book of Shadows. *Forgotten Books.* ISBN 978-1605069333.

Ingenito, T. (2021). *The evolution of spears.* https://www.sutori.com/story/the-evolution-of-spears--sVeTKrpCsnoZd-PUau4fca9Ru

Kahn, N. (2020). Mark your calendar for September's practical new moon. *Bustle Magazine.* https://www.bustle.com/life/next-new-moon-calendar

McDermott, N. (2019). Car crashes are more common during a full moon with men particularly vulnerable to the 'werewolf effect', research reveals. *The Sun.* https://www.thesun.co.uk/motors/9048871/car-crashes-common-during-full-moon/

OtherWorldly.com. (2019). *The witch's cauldron: Origins, magic & how to use a cauldron today*. https://otherworldly-oracle.com/witchs-cauldron/

Poppick, L. (2013). 6 Wild ways the moon affects animals. *Live Science Magazine*. https://www.livescience.com/37928-ways-the-moon-affects-animals.html

www.ingramcontent.com/pod-product-compliance
Lightning Source LLC
Chambersburg PA
CBHW021446070526
44577CB00002B/271